Cookie Dough
FUN

Publications International, Ltd.
Favorite Brand Name Recipes at www.fbnr.com

Recipe Development: Bev Bennett, ErdaTek, Inc., Alison Reich and Marcia Stanley

Photography on pages 11, 17, 23, 25, 29, 51, 55, 63, 75, 81, 83, 87, 93, 105, 109, 111, 115, 127, 133, 147, 151, 155, 165, 169, 171, 175, 183, 185, 193 and 197 by Proffitt Photography Ltd., Chicago.
Photography on pages 9, 15, 19, 31, 33, 35, 47, 49, 53, 57, 59, 61, 77, 79, 85, 91, 95, 97, 99, 103, 107, 119, 123, 149, 153, 157, 159, 163, 189 and 203 by Stephen Hamilton Photographics, Inc.

Pictured on the front cover: Citrus Easter Chicks *(page 184).*
Pictured on the back cover *(left to right):* Sparkling Magic Wands *(page 74),* Springtime Nests *(page 180)* and Brown-Eyed Susans *(page 28).*

ISBN-13: 978-1-4127-8327-9
ISBN-10: 1-4127-8327-5

Library of Congress Control Number: 2004100671

Manufactured in China.

8 7 6 5 4 3 2 1

Microwave Cooking: Microwave ovens vary in wattage. Use the cooking times as guidelines and check for doneness before adding more time.

Preparation/Cooking Times: Preparation times are based on the approximate amount of time required to assemble the recipe before cooking, baking, chilling or serving. These times include preparation steps such as measuring, chopping and mixing. The fact that some preparations and cooking can be done simultaneously is taken into account. Preparation of optional ingredients and serving suggestions is not included.

Contents

Basic Cookie Tips

- Read the entire recipe before beginning to make sure you have all the necessary ingredients, baking utensils and supplies.

- Unless the recipe states otherwise, all purchased cookie dough should be well chilled before using. Work with the recommended portion of dough called for and refrigerate the remaining dough until needed.

- Measure all the ingredients accurately and assemble them in the order they are called for in the recipe.

- Most purchased cookie dough expands considerably when baked. Always leave 2 inches between unbaked cookies when placing them on the cookie sheet, unless the recipe directs otherwise.

- Follow the recipe directions and baking times exactly. Check for doneness using the test given in the recipe. Most cookies bake quickly, so check them at the minimum baking time, then watch carefully to make sure they do not burn.

- Cookies that are uniform in size and shape will finish baking at the same time.

Making Patterns for Cutouts

When a pattern for a cutout cookie is to be used only once, make the pattern out of waxed paper. Using the photo or diagram as a guide, draw the pattern pieces on waxed paper. Cut the pieces out and place them on the rolled-out cookie dough. Carefully cut around the pattern pieces with a sharp knife. Remove the pattern pieces from the dough and discard. Continue as directed in the recipe.

For patterns that are to be used more than once, make the pattern more durable by using clean, lightweight cardboard or poster board. Using the photo or diagram as a guide, draw the pattern pieces on the cardboard. Cut the pieces out and lightly spray one side with nonstick cooking spray. Place the pattern pieces, sprayed side down, on the rolled-out dough; cut around them with a sharp knife. Reuse the pattern pieces to make as many cutouts as needed.

Decorating Ideas

Chocolate Drizzle

Melted chocolate or white chocolate provides a pretty finishing touch to many baked goods. Simply drizzle melted chocolate with a spoon or fork over baked goods. The contrast of a white chocolate drizzle on a dark chocolate cookie is sure to draw attention.

Powdered Sugar Glaze

Plain cookies get a boost of sweetness with a powdered sugar glaze. Use the glaze white or tint it with food coloring to fit the occasion. Simply combine 1 cup sifted powdered sugar and 5 teaspoons milk in a small bowl. Add ½ teaspoon vanilla extract or other flavoring, if desired. Stir until smooth and tint with food coloring, if desired. If the glaze is too thin, add additional powdered sugar; if it is too thick, add additional milk, ½ teaspoon at a time.

Toasted Nuts

A sprinkle of chopped nuts is a great topping for frosted treats. To toast, spread nuts in a thin layer on an ungreased cookie sheet. Bake in a preheated 325°F oven 8 to 10 minutes or until golden, stirring occasionally to promote even browning and prevent burning. Toasted nuts will become darker and crisper as they cool. Always allow nuts to cool before using.

Toasted Coconut

Coconut sprinkled on frosted brownies or cookies adds a distinctive appearance and flavor. To toast coconut, spread a thin layer of flaked coconut on a cookie sheet. Bake in a preheated 325°F oven 7 to 10 minutes. Shake the pan or stir the coconut occasionally during baking to promote even browning and prevent burning.

Tinted Coconut

Tinted coconut is a festive and colorful decoration. To tint coconut, dilute a few drops of liquid food coloring with ½ teaspoon milk or water in a small bowl. Add 1 to 1⅓ cups flaked coconut and toss with a fork until the coconut is evenly tinted.

Melting Chocolate

Make sure the utensils you use for melting chocolate are completely dry. Moisture makes chocolate become stiff and grainy. If this happens, add ½ teaspoon shortening (not butter) for each ounce of chocolate and stir until smooth. Chocolate scorches easily and cannot be used once it is scorched. Use one of the following methods for successful melting.

Double Boiler: This is the safest method because it prevents scorching. Place the chocolate in the top of a double boiler or in a bowl over hot, not boiling, water; stir until smooth. (Make sure the water remains just below a simmer and is one inch below the top pan.) Be careful that no steam or water gets into the chocolate.

Direct Heat: Place the chocolate in a heavy saucepan and melt it over very low heat, stirring constantly. Remove the chocolate from the heat as soon as it is melted. Be sure to watch the chocolate carefully since it is easily scorched with this method.

Microwave Oven: Place 4 to 6 unwrapped 1-ounce squares of chocolate or 1 cup of chocolate chips in a small microwavable bowl. Microwave at HIGH (100% power) for 1 to 1½ minutes. Stir after 1 minute and at 30-second intervals after the first minute. Repeat the procedure as necessary to melt the chocolate. Be sure to stir the microwaved chocolate because it can retain its original shape even when melted.

Storing Cookies

- Store soft and crisp cookies separately at room temperature to prevent changes in texture and flavor.
- Keep soft cookies in airtight containers. If they begin to dry out, add a piece of apple or bread to the container to help them retain moisture.
- Store crisp cookies in containers with loose-fitting lids to prevent moisture build-up. If they become soggy, heat undecorated cookies in a 300°F oven for 3 to 5 minutes to restore crispness.
- Store cookies with sticky glazes, fragile decorations and icings in single layers between sheets of waxed paper.
- Bar cookies and brownies may be stored in their own baking pan, covered with aluminum foil or plastic wrap when cool.
- Freeze baked cookies in airtight containers or freezer bags for up to 6 months. Thaw them unwrapped at room temperature.

Cookie Sundae Cups

1 package (18 ounces) refrigerated chocolate chip cookie
   dough
6 cups ice cream, any flavor
1¼ cups ice cream topping, any flavor
   Whipped cream
   Colored sprinkles

1. Preheat oven to 350°F. Lightly grease 18 (2½-inch) muffin pan cups.

2. Remove dough from wrapper. Shape dough into 18 balls; press onto bottoms and up sides of prepared muffin cups.

3. Bake 14 to 18 minutes or until golden brown. Cool in muffin cups 10 minutes. Remove to wire rack; cool completely.

4. Place ⅓ cup ice cream in each cookie cup. Drizzle with ice cream topping. Top with whipped cream and colored sprinkles. *Makes 1½ dozen desserts*

Burger Bliss

Buns

1 package (18 ounces) refrigerated sugar cookie dough
½ cup creamy peanut butter
⅓ cup all-purpose flour
¼ cup packed light brown sugar
½ teaspoon vanilla
Beaten egg white and sesame seeds (optional)

Burgers

½ (18-ounce) package refrigerated sugar cookie dough
3 tablespoons unsweetened cocoa powder
2 tablespoons packed light brown sugar
½ teaspoon vanilla
Red, yellow and green decorating icings

1. Preheat oven to 350°F. Grease cookie sheets. For buns, remove dough from wrapper; place in large bowl. Let stand at room temperature 15 minutes. Add peanut butter, flour, brown sugar and vanilla to dough; beat until blended. Shape into 48 (1-inch) balls; place 2 inches apart on cookie sheets.

2. Bake 14 minutes or until browned. If desired, remove from oven after 10 minutes; brush with egg white and sprinkle with sesame seeds. Return to oven; bake 4 minutes. Cool on cookie sheets 2 to 3 minutes. Remove to wire racks; cool completely.

3. For burgers, remove half of dough from wrapper. (Reserve remaining dough for another use.) Beat dough, cocoa, brown sugar and vanilla in bowl until blended. Shape into 24 (1-inch) balls; place 2 inches apart on cookie sheets. Flatten cookies to ¼-inch thickness with a diameter slightly larger than buns.

4. Bake 12 minutes or until firm. Cool on cookie sheets 2 to 3 minutes. Remove to wire rack; cool completely.

5. To assemble, use icing to attach burgers to flat sides of 24 buns; pipe red, yellow and green icings on burgers. Top with remaining buns.   *Makes 2 dozen sandwich cookies*

Burger Bliss

Pretty Posies

1 package (20 ounces) refrigerated sugar cookie dough
Orange and purple or blue food colorings
1 tablespoon colored sprinkles

1. Remove dough from wrapper. Reserve ⅚ of dough. Combine remaining dough, orange food coloring and sprinkles in small bowl; beat at medium speed of electric mixer until well blended. Shape into 7½ inch log. Wrap in plastic wrap; refrigerate 30 minutes or until firm.

2. Combine reserved dough and purple food coloring in large bowl; beat at medium speed of electric mixer until well blended. Shape dough into disc. Wrap in plastic wrap; refrigerate 30 minutes or until firm.

3. Roll out purple dough on waxed paper to 6×7½-inch rectangle. Place orange log in center of rectangle. Fold purple edges up and around orange log; press seam together. Roll gently to form smooth log. Wrap waxed paper around dough and twist ends to secure. Freeze log 20 minutes.

4. Preheat oven to 350°F. Lightly grease cookie sheets. Remove waxed paper from dough log. Cut log into ¼-inch slices. Place 2 inches apart on prepared cookie sheets. Using 2½-inch flower-shaped cookie cutter, cut slices into flowers; remove and discard dough scraps.

5. Bake 15 to 17 minutes or until edges are lightly browned. Remove to wire rack; cool completely.

Makes about 1½ dozen cookies

Pretty Posies

Cookie Fondue

Cookie Dippers
  1 package (18 ounces) refrigerated oatmeal raisin cookie
    dough
  1 cup powdered sugar
  1 egg

Chocolate Sauce
  ½ cup semisweet chocolate chips
  ¼ cup heavy cream

White Chocolate Sauce
  ½ cup white chocolate chips
  ¼ cup heavy cream

Strawberry-Marshmallow Sauce
  ¼ cup strawberry syrup
  ¼ cup marshmallow creme

1. For dippers, preheat oven to 350°F. Grease cookie sheets. Remove dough from wrapper; place in large bowl. Let dough stand at room temperature about 15 minutes. Add powdered sugar and egg to dough; beat until well blended. Drop dough by teaspoonfuls onto prepared cookie sheets. Bake 8 minutes or until edges are lightly browned. Cool on cookie sheets 5 minutes. Remove to wire rack; cool completely.

2. For chocolate sauce, mix semisweet chocolate chips and cream in microwavable bowl. Heat at HIGH (100% power) 20 seconds; stir. Heat at HIGH at additional 20-second intervals until melted and smooth; stir well after each interval. For white chocolate sauce, repeat with white chocolate chips and cream.

3. For strawberry-marshmallow sauce, mix strawberry syrup and marshmallow creme in small bowl; stir until smooth. Serve cookie dippers with sauces.   *Makes 2½ dozen cookies*

Hint: Serve sauces in small bowls along with small bowls of chopped nuts, coconut and dried cranberries for double dipping.

Cookie Fondue

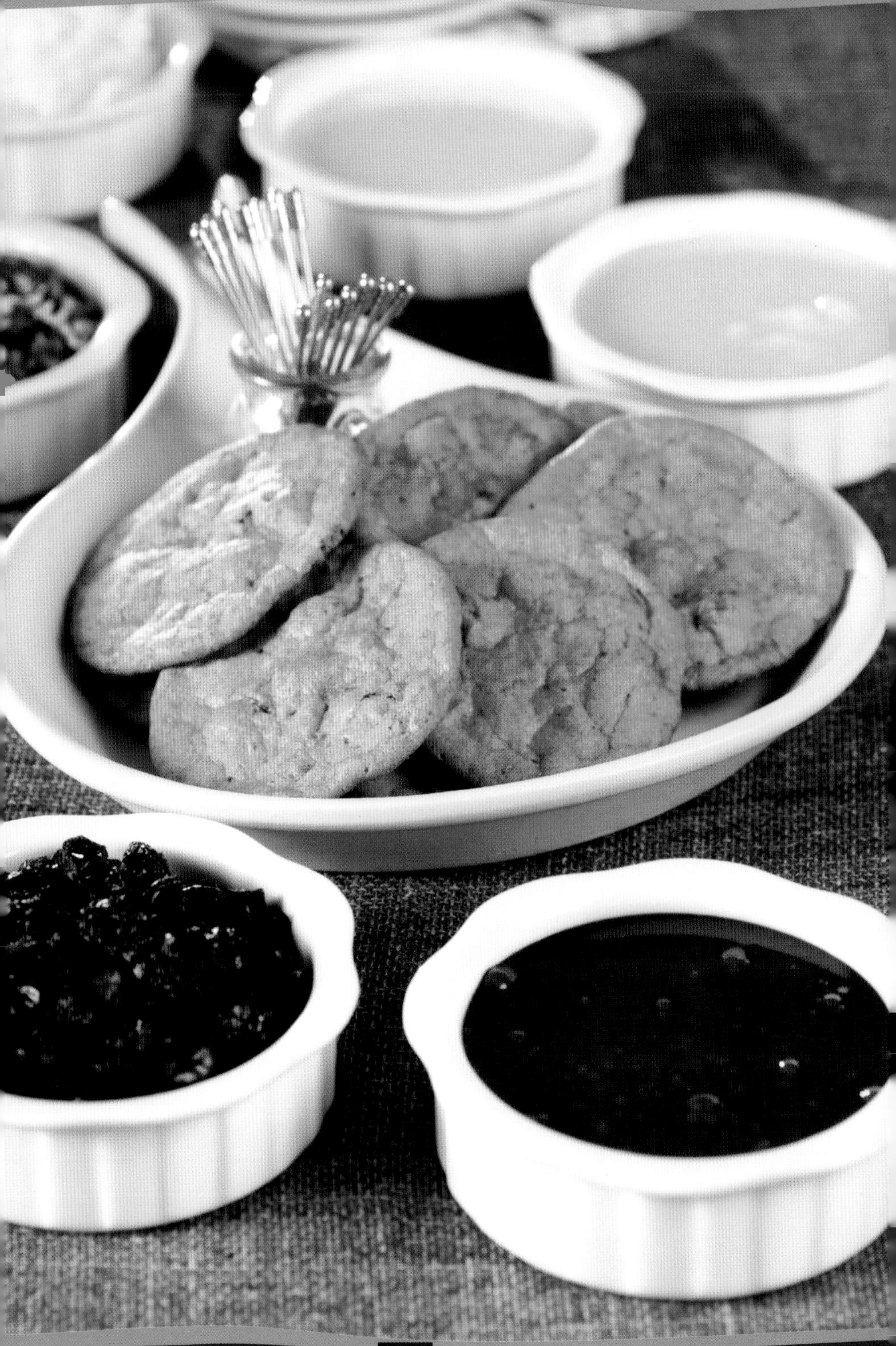

Chocolate Truffle Cookies

1 package (18 ounces) refrigerated sugar cookie dough
⅓ cup unsweetened cocoa powder
1 tablespoon powdered sugar
½ teaspoon vanilla
1 package (12 ounces) milk chocolate-covered chewy
    chocolate caramel candies (¾-inch squares)
¾ cup semisweet chocolate chips
    Colored sprinkles

1. Preheat oven to 325°F. Line cookie sheets with parchment paper. Remove dough from wrapper; place in large bowl. Let dough stand at room temperature about 15 minutes.

2. Add cocoa, powdered sugar and vanilla to dough; beat at medium speed of electric mixer until well blended.

3. Shape about 2 teaspoons dough into ball; wrap ball around 1 caramel candy. Repeat with remaining dough and candies. Place filled balls 2 inches apart on prepared cookie sheets. Bake 12 to 15 minutes or until set. Remove to wire rack; cool completely.

4. Place wire rack over waxed paper. Place chocolate chips in small microwavable bowl. Microwave at HIGH (100% power) 1 to 1½ minutes. Stir after 1 minute and at 30-second intervals after first minute until chips are melted and smooth. Spoon small amount of chocolate on top of each cookie; top with sprinkles. Let stand on wire rack until set. Store in refrigerator.

Makes about 3 dozen cookies

Twisty Sticks

1 package (18 ounces) refrigerated sugar cookie dough
6 tablespoons all-purpose flour, divided
1 tablespoon unsweetened cocoa powder
2 tablespoons creamy peanut butter
1 cup semisweet chocolate chips
1 tablespoon shortening
Colored sprinkles and finely chopped peanuts

1. Remove dough from wrapper. Divide dough in half; place in separate medium bowls. Let dough stand at room temperature about 15 minutes.

2. Add 3 tablespoons flour and cocoa powder to one dough half; beat at medium speed of electric mixer until well blended. Wrap in plastic wrap; refrigerate at least 1 hour.

3. Add remaining 3 tablespoons flour and peanut butter to remaining dough; beat at medium speed of electric mixer until well blended. Wrap in plastic wrap; refrigerate at least 1 hour.

4. Preheat oven to 350°F. Divide chocolate dough into 30 equal pieces. Divide peanut butter dough into 30 equal pieces. Shape each dough piece into 4-inch-long rope on lightly floured surface. For each cookie, twist 1 chocolate rope and 1 peanut butter rope together. Place 2 inches apart on ungreased cookie sheets. Bake 7 to 10 minutes or until set. Remove to wire rack; cool completely.

5. Meanwhile, combine chocolate chips and shortening in small microwavable bowl. Microwave at HIGH (100% power) 1 to 1½ minutes. Stir after 1 minute and at 30-second intervals after first minute until chips are melted and smooth Spread chocolate on 1 end of each cookie; top with sprinkles and peanuts as desired. Place on waxed paper. Let stand 30 minutes or until set.   *Makes 2½ dozen cookies*

Twisty Sticks

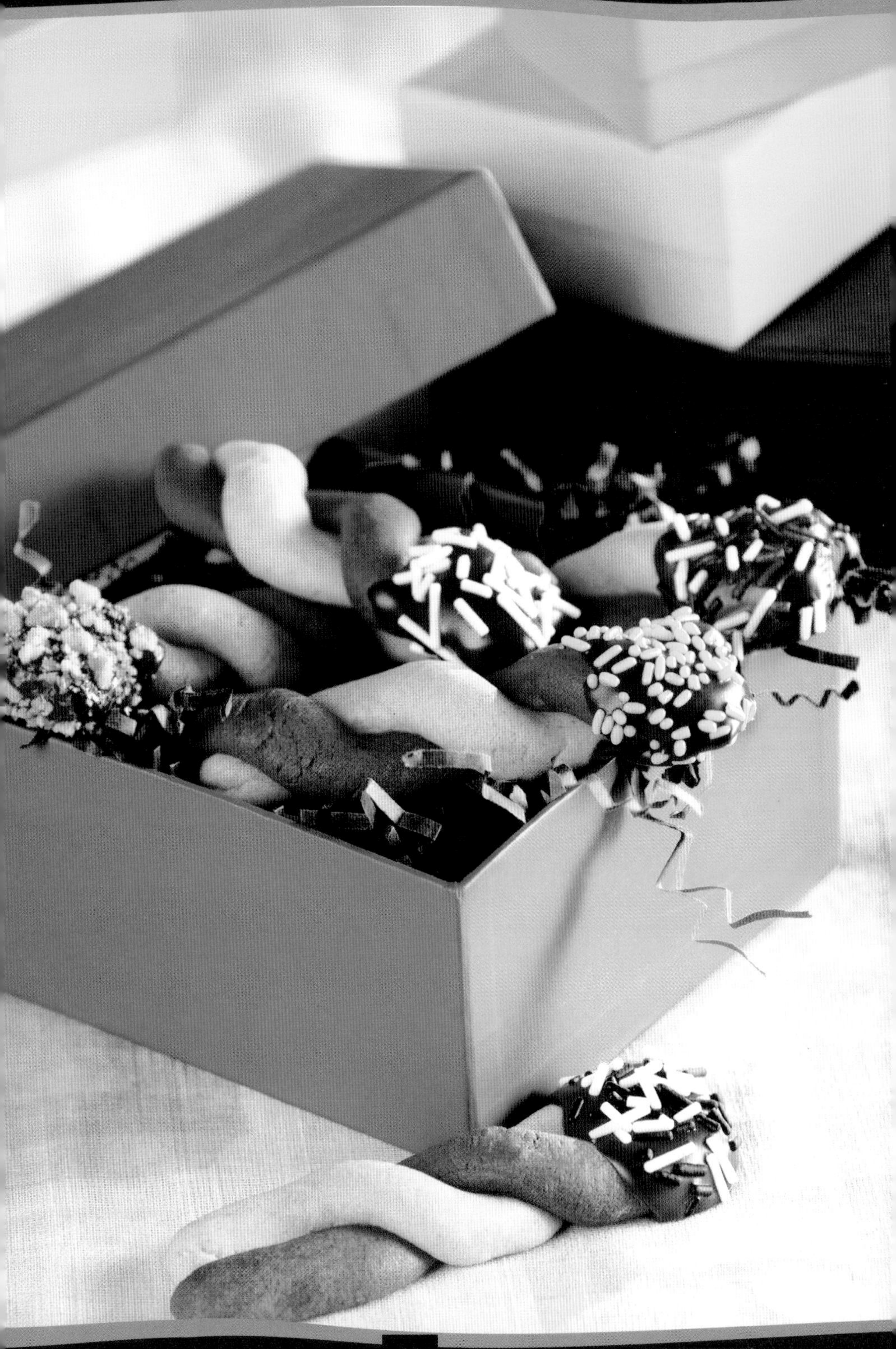

S'Mores on a Stick

1 (14-ounce) can EAGLE BRAND® Sweetened Condensed Milk (NOT evaporated milk), divided
1½ cups milk chocolate mini chips, divided
1 cup miniature marshmallows
11 whole graham crackers, halved crosswise
Toppings: chopped peanuts, mini candy-coated chocolate pieces, sprinkles

1. Microwave half of Eagle Brand in microwave-safe bowl at HIGH (100% power) 1½ minutes. Stir in 1 cup chips until smooth; stir in marshmallows.

2. Spread chocolate mixture evenly by heaping tablespoonfuls onto 11 graham cracker halves. Top with remaining graham cracker halves; place on waxed paper.

3. Microwave remaining Eagle Brand at HIGH (100% power) 1½ minutes; stir in remaining ½ cup chips, stirring until smooth. Drizzle mixture over cookies and sprinkle with desired toppings.

4. Let stand for 2 hours; insert a wooden craft stick into center of each cookie.   *Makes 11 servings*

Prep Time: 10 minutes
Cook Time: 3 minutes

S'Mores on a Stick

Cookie Nuggets

35 rich round crackers
**1 package (18 ounces) refrigerated chocolate chip cookie
dough with peanut butter filling in squares or rounds
(20 count)**
Honey and strawberry or raspberry jam

1. Preheat oven to 350°F. Grease cookie sheets.

2. Remove dough from wrapper; place in large bowl. Let dough stand at room temperature about 15 minutes. Meanwhile, place crackers in resealable plastic food storage bag; seal bag. Crush crackers with rolling pin until fine crumbs are formed. Reserve ½ cup crumbs.

3. Add remaining crumbs to dough in bowl; beat at medium speed of electric mixer until well blended. Shape 2 rounded teaspoonfuls of dough into oval; flatten slightly. Roll in reserved crumbs; place on prepared cookie sheets. Pinch in sides of oval to make cookie resemble chicken nugget. Repeat with remaining dough and crumbs.

4. Bake 8 to 10 minutes or until set. Cool on cookie sheets 10 minutes. Remove to wire rack; cool completely.

5. Serve cookies with honey and jam for dipping.

Makes about 2½ dozen cookies

Tip: If dough becomes too soft to shape, refrigerate 15 minutes.

Cookie Nuggets

Root Beer Floats

1 package (18 ounces) refrigerated sugar cookie dough
3 tablespoons all-purpose flour
1½ teaspoons root beer concentrate
 Root Beer Royal Icing (page 26)
 Assorted food colorings
3 cups mini marshmallows
 White sugar crystals

1. Preheat oven to 350°F. Grease cookie sheets.

2. Remove dough from wrapper; place in large bowl. Let dough stand at room temperature about 15 minutes.

3. Add flour and root beer concentrate to dough; beat at medium speed of electric mixer until well blended. Divide dough in half. Wrap each half in plastic wrap; freeze 30 minutes.

4. Roll 1 dough half on lightly floured surface to ¼-inch thickness. Cut into 2¾×3-inch rectangles. Cut ⅜-inch slice from one short end of each rectangle; set aside. Cut slight curve into remaining short ends to make rounded bottoms of mugs. Place cutouts 2 inches apart on prepared cookie sheets. Use ⅜-inch dough slices to create mug handles. Repeat with remaining dough half.

5. Bake 8 to 10 minutes or until just set. Cool on cookie sheets 10 minutes. Remove to wire rack; cool completely.

6. For each cookie, cut about 10 mini marshmallows into halves and quarters. Prepare Root Beer Royal Icing; reserve ⅓ cup icing. Tint remaining icing with food colorings as desired. Spread tinted icing on cookies.

continued on page 26

Root Beer Floats

Root Beer Floats, continued

7. Place reserved white icing in resealable plastic food storage bag; cut off tiny corner of bag. Pipe along top edges of cookies and down sides. Place mini marshmallow pieces on icing. Sprinkle cookies with sugar crystals. Let stand 15 minutes or until icing is set.   *Makes about 2 dozen cookies*

Root Beer Royal Icing

2 egg whites,* at room temperature
3½ to 4½ cups sifted powdered sugar, divided
¼ teaspoon root beer concentrate

*Use only grade A clean, uncracked eggs.

1. Beat egg whites in small bowl at high speed of electric mixer until foamy.

2. Gradually add 3½ cups powdered sugar and root beer concentrate. Beat at low speed of electric mixer until moistened. Increase speed to high and beat until icing is stiff, adding additional powdered sugar if needed.

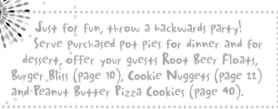

Just for fun, throw a backwards party! Serve purchased pot pies for dinner and for dessert, offer your guests Root Beer Floats, Burger Bliss (page 10), Cookie Nuggets (page 22) and Peanut Butter Pizza Cookies (page 40).

Peanut Butter and Chocolate Cookie Sandwich Cookies

½ cup REESE'S® Peanut Butter Chips
3 tablespoons plus ½ cup butter, softened and divided
1¼ cups sugar, divided
¼ cup light corn syrup
1 egg
1 teaspoon vanilla extract
2 cups plus 2 tablespoons all-purpose flour, divided
2 teaspoons baking soda
¼ teaspoon salt
½ cup HERSHEY®S Cocoa
5 tablespoons butter or margarine, melted
Additional sugar
About 2 dozen large marshmallows

1. Heat oven to 350°F. Melt peanut butter chips and 3 tablespoons softened butter in small saucepan over very low heat. Remove from heat; cool slightly.

2. Beat remaining ½ cup softened butter and 1 cup sugar in large bowl until fluffy. Add corn syrup, egg and vanilla; blend thoroughly. Stir together 2 cups flour, baking soda and salt; add to butter mixture, blending well. Remove 1¼ cups batter and place in small bowl; with wooden spoon, stir in remaining 2 tablespoons flour and melted peanut butter chip mixture.

3. Blend cocoa, remaining ¼ cup sugar and 5 tablespoons melted butter into remaining batter. Refrigerate both batters 5 to 10 minutes or until firm enough to handle. Roll dough into 1-inch balls; roll in sugar. Place on ungreased cookie sheet.

4. Bake 10 to 11 minutes or until set. Cool slightly; remove from cookie sheet to wire rack. Cool completely. Place 1 marshmallow on flat side of 1 chocolate cookie. Microwave at MEDIUM (50%) 10 seconds or until marshmallow is softened. Place peanut butter cookie over marshmallow; press down. Repeat for remaining cookies.   *Makes 2 dozen sandwich cookies*

Brown-Eyed Susans

1 package (18 ounces) refrigerated sugar cookie dough
3 tablespoons unsweetened Dutch process cocoa powder
¼ cup all-purpose flour
1½ teaspoons banana extract
Yellow food coloring

1. Preheat oven to 350°F. Lightly grease cookie sheets.

2. Remove dough from wrapper; reserve ⅔ of dough. Place remaining ⅓ dough in medium bowl; let stand at room temperature about 15 minutes.

3. For flower centers, add cocoa to dough in bowl; beat at medium speed of electric mixer until well blended. Divide cocoa dough into 30 pieces; shape into balls. Place balls about 4 inches apart on prepared cookie sheets.

4. For flower petals, combine reserved dough, flour, banana extract and food coloring in medium bowl; beat at medium speed of electric mixer until well blended and evenly colored. Divide dough into 30 pieces. Shape each piece into 6 ovals; place in circle around center ball on cookie sheet, leaving about ¼-inch space between petals and center ball. Pinch outside ends of yellow ovals to points for petal shapes. Repeat with remaining yellow pieces.

5. Bake 7 to 9 minutes or until firm but not browned. Cool completely on cookie sheets.   *Makes 2½ dozen cookies*

Note: "Dutch process" cocoa is unsweetened cocoa that has been treated with an alkali, giving it a darker appearance and a slightly less bitter flavor.

Brown-Eyed Susans

Rocky Road Sandwiches

**1 package (18 ounces) refrigerated chocolate chip cookie
  dough**
¼ cup unsweetened cocoa powder
1 cup marshmallow creme
6 ounces (⅔ cup) cream cheese, softened
1 cup finely chopped nuts

1. Preheat oven to 350°F. Grease cookie sheets.

2. Remove dough from wrapper; place in large bowl. Let dough stand at room temperature about 15 minutes.

3. Add cocoa to dough; beat at medium speed of electric mixer until well blended. Drop dough by rounded teaspoonfuls onto prepared cookie sheets.

4. Bake 8 to 10 minutes or until set and no longer shiny. Remove to wire rack; cool completely.

5. For filling, combine marshmallow creme and cream cheese in medium bowl; beat at medium speed of electric mixer until well blended. Place 1 tablespoon filling on flat side of cookie. Top with second cookie; press down to allow filling to squeeze out slightly between cookies. Roll filled edge in chopped nuts. Repeat with remaining cookies, filling and nuts.

Makes about 1½ dozen sandwich cookies

Watermelon Slices

2 packages (18 ounces each) refrigerated sugar cookie dough, divided
½ cup all-purpose flour, divided
Green and red food colorings
Mini chocolate chips

1. Remove both sugar doughs from wrappers; place in separate medium bowls. Let stand at room temperature about 15 minutes. Add ¼ cup flour and green food coloring to dough in one bowl; beat at medium speed of electric mixer until well blended and evenly colored. Wrap in plastic wrap; refrigerate about 2 hours.

2. Add remaining ¼ cup flour and red food coloring to dough in remaining bowl; beat at medium speed of electric mixer until well blended and evenly colored. Shape into 9-inch-long log. Sprinkle with flour to minimize sticking, if necessary. Wrap in plastic wrap; refrigerate about 2 hours.

3. Remove green dough from refrigerator. Roll between sheets of waxed paper to 9×8-inch rectangle. Remove plastic wrap from red dough log; place in center of green rectangle.

4. Fold green edges up and around red dough log; press seam together. Roll gently to form smooth log. Wrap in plastic wrap. Freeze 30 minutes.

5. Preheat oven to 350°F. Remove waxed paper. Cut log into ⅜-inch-thick slices. Cut each slice in half. Place 2 inches apart on ungreased cookie sheets. Gently re-shape, if necessary. Press several mini chocolate chips into each slice for watermelon seeds. Bake 8 to 11 minutes or until set. Cool on cookie sheets 1 minute. Remove to wire rack; cool completely.

Makes about 5 dozen cookies

Brownie Bites

1 package (18 ounces) refrigerated chocolate chip cookie
  dough with fudge filling in squares or rounds
  (20 count)
¼ cup unsweetened cocoa powder
1½ teaspoons vanilla, divided
1 package (18 ounces) refrigerated chocolate chip cookie
  dough
4 ounces (½ cup) cream cheese, softened
1 cup sifted powdered sugar

1. Grease 30 mini (1¾-inch) muffin pan cups. Remove chocolate chip and fudge cookie dough from wrapper; place in large bowl. Let dough stand at room temperature about 15 minutes.

2. Add cocoa and ½ teaspoon vanilla to dough in bowl; beat at medium speed of electric mixer until well blended. Shape dough into 30 balls; press onto bottoms and up sides of prepared muffin cups. Refrigerate 1 hour.

3. Preheat oven to 350°F. Remove chocolate chip cookie dough from wrapper. Shape into 30 balls. Place each chocolate chip ball into dough-lined muffin cups. Gently flatten tops if necessary. Bake 14 to 16 minutes. Cool in pans 10 minutes. Remove to wire rack; cool completely.

4. Combine cream cheese and remaining 1 teaspoon vanilla in medium bowl. Beat at medium speed of electric mixer, gradually adding powdered sugar until frosting is light and fluffy. Spoon heaping teaspoonful frosting onto each cookie.

Makes 2½ dozen cookies

Note: These cookies are best served the day they are made; leftovers should be refrigerated.

Congrats Grad!

1 package (18 ounces) refrigerated sugar cookie dough
¼ cup *each* all-purpose flour and creamy peanut butter
1 cup mini chocolate chips
   Granulated sugar
48 small gumdrops to match school colors
   Cookie Glaze (recipe follows)
   Food colorings to match school colors
12 graham cracker squares

1. Preheat oven to 350°F. Grease 12 (2½-inch) muffin cups. Remove dough from wrapper. Beat dough, flour and peanut butter in large bowl until well blended. Stir in chocolate chips. Shape dough into 12 balls; press onto bottoms and up sides of prepared muffin cups.

2. Bake 15 to 18 minutes or until browned; let cool in pan on wire rack 10 minutes. Remove from pan; cool completely.

3. Sprinkle sugar on waxed paper. For each tassel, slightly flatten 3 gumdrops. Place gumdrops, with ends overlapping slightly, on sugared surface. Sprinkle with additional sugar as needed. Roll flattened gumdrops into 3×1-inch piece with rolling pin, turning piece over often to coat with sugar. Trim and discard edges of gumdrop piece. Cut piece into 2½×¼-inch strips. Cut bottom part into several lengthwise strips to form fringe.

4. Prepare Cookie Glaze; tint desired color. Place cookies upside down on wire racks set over waxed paper. Spread glaze over cookies to cover. Spread glaze over graham crackers; set crackers on top of cookie. Place tassel on each cap; top with gumdrop. Let stand 40 minutes or until glaze is set.

Makes 1 dozen large cookies

Cookie Glaze: Combine 4 cups powdered sugar and 6 to 8 tablespoons milk, 1 tablespoon at a time, to make medium-thick pourable glaze.

Congrats Grad!

Double Chocolate Sandwich Cookies

1 package (18 ounces) refrigerated sugar cookie dough
1 bar (3½ to 4 ounces) bittersweet chocolate, chopped
2 teaspoons butter
¾ cup milk chocolate chips

1. Preheat oven to 350°F. Remove dough from wrapper, keeping in log shape.

2. Cut dough into ¼-inch-thick slices. Arrange slices 2 inches apart on ungreased cookie sheets. Cut centers out of half the cookies using 1-inch round cookie cutter.

3. Bake 10 to 12 minutes or until edges are lightly browned. Let stand on cookie sheets 2 minutes. Remove to wire rack; cool completely.

4. Place bittersweet chocolate and butter in heavy small saucepan. Heat over low heat, stirring frequently, until chocolate is melted. Spread chocolate over flat sides of cookies without holes. Immediately top each with cutout cookie.

5. Place milk chocolate chips in resealable plastic food storage bag; seal bag. Microwave at MEDIUM (50% power) 1½ minutes. Turn bag over; microwave 1 to 1½ minutes or until melted. Knead bag until chocolate is smooth.

6. Cut tiny corner off bag; drizzle chocolate decoratively over sandwich cookies. Let stand until chocolate is set, about 30 minutes.   *Makes 16 sandwich cookies*

Double Chocolate Sandwich Cookies

Peanut Butter Pizza Cookies

1¼ cups firmly packed light brown sugar
¾ cup JIF® Creamy Peanut Butter
½ CRISCO® Stick or ½ cup CRISCO® all-vegetable shortening
3 tablespoons milk
1 tablespoon vanilla
1 egg
1¾ cups all-purpose flour
¾ teaspoon salt
¾ teaspoon baking soda
8 ounces white baking chocolate, chopped
Decorative candies

1. Heat oven to 375°F. Place sheets of foil on countertop for cooling cookies.

2. Combine brown sugar, peanut butter, shortening, milk and vanilla in large bowl. Beat at medium speed of electric mixer until well blended. Add egg. Beat just until blended.

3. Combine flour, salt and baking soda. Add to creamed mixture at low speed. Mix just until blended.

4. Divide dough in half. Form each half into a ball. Place 1 ball of dough onto center of ungreased pizza pan or baking sheet. Spread dough with fingers to form 12-inch circle. Repeat with remaining ball of dough.

5. Bake one baking sheet at a time at 375°F for 10 to 12 minutes, or until lightly browned. *Do not overbake.* Cool 2 minutes on baking sheet. Remove with spatula to foil to cool completely.

6. Place white chocolate in shallow microwave-safe bowl. Microwave on 100% (HIGH) for 30 seconds. Stir. Repeat at 30-second intervals until white chocolate is melted.

7. Spread melted white chocolate on center of cooled cookies to within ½ inch of edge. Decorate with candies. Let set completely. Cut into wedges. *Makes 2 pizzas*

Peanut Butter Pizza Cookie

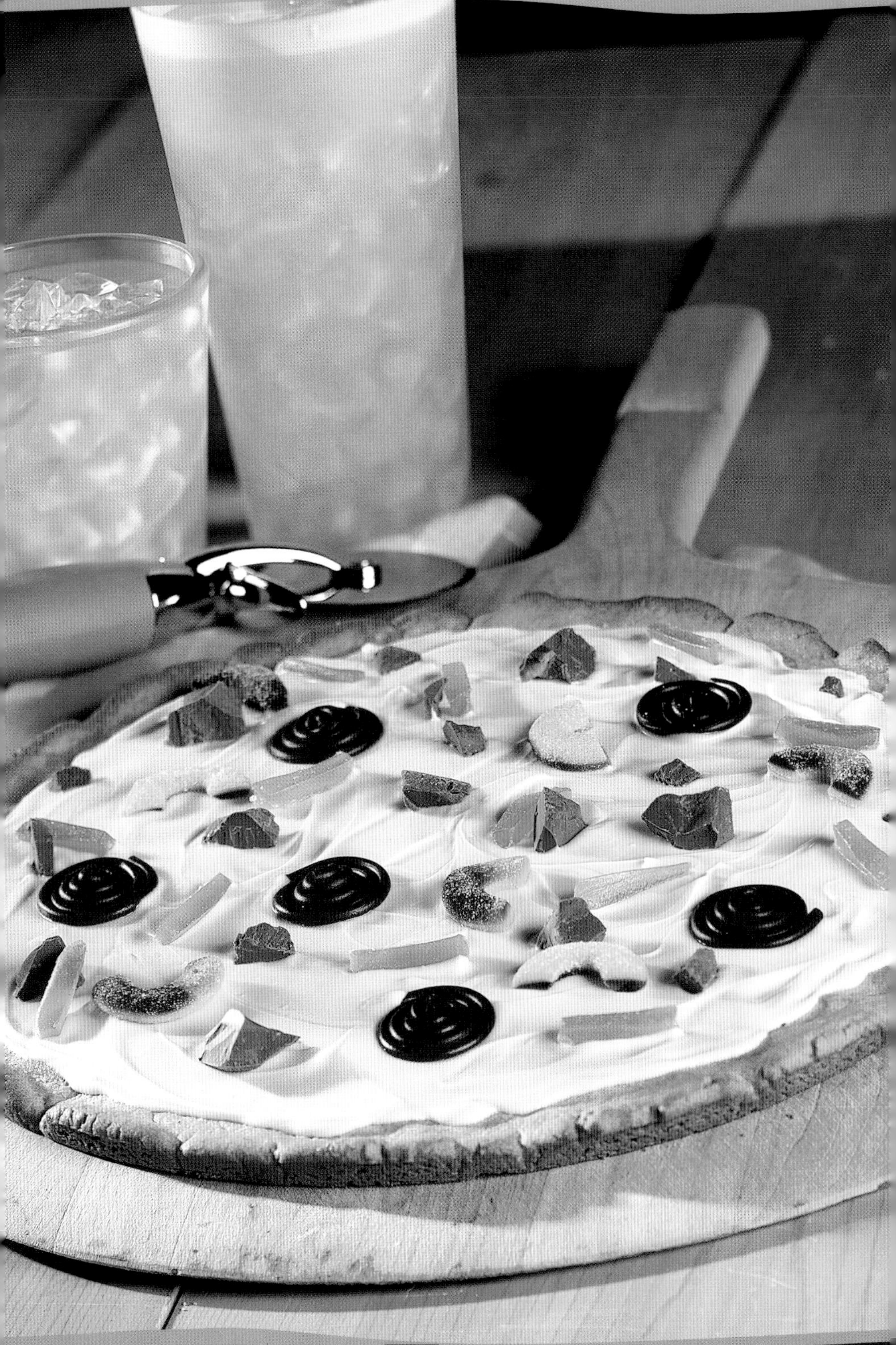

Greeting Card Cookies

½ cup (1 stick) butter or margarine, softened
¾ cup sugar
1 egg
1 teaspoon vanilla extract
1½ cups all-purpose flour
⅓ cup HERSHEY®S Cocoa
½ teaspoon baking powder
½ teaspoon baking soda
¼ teaspoon salt
   Decorative Frosting (page 44)

1. Beat butter, sugar, egg and vanilla in large bowl until fluffy. Stir together flour, cocoa, baking powder, baking soda and salt; add to butter mixture, blending well. Refrigerate about 1 hour or until firm enough to roll. Cut cardboard rectangle for pattern, 2½×4 inches; wrap in plastic wrap.

2. Heat oven to 350°F. Lightly grease cookie sheet. On lightly floured board or between two pieces of wax paper, roll out half of dough to ¼-inch thickness. For each cookie, place pattern on dough; cut through dough around pattern with sharp paring knife. (Save dough trimmings and reroll for remaining cookies.) Carefully place cutouts on prepared cookie sheet.

3. Bake 8 to 10 minutes or until set. Cool 1 minute on cookie sheet. (If cookies have lost their shape, trim irregular edges while cookies are still hot.) Carefully transfer to wire rack. Repeat procedure with remaining dough.

continued on page 44

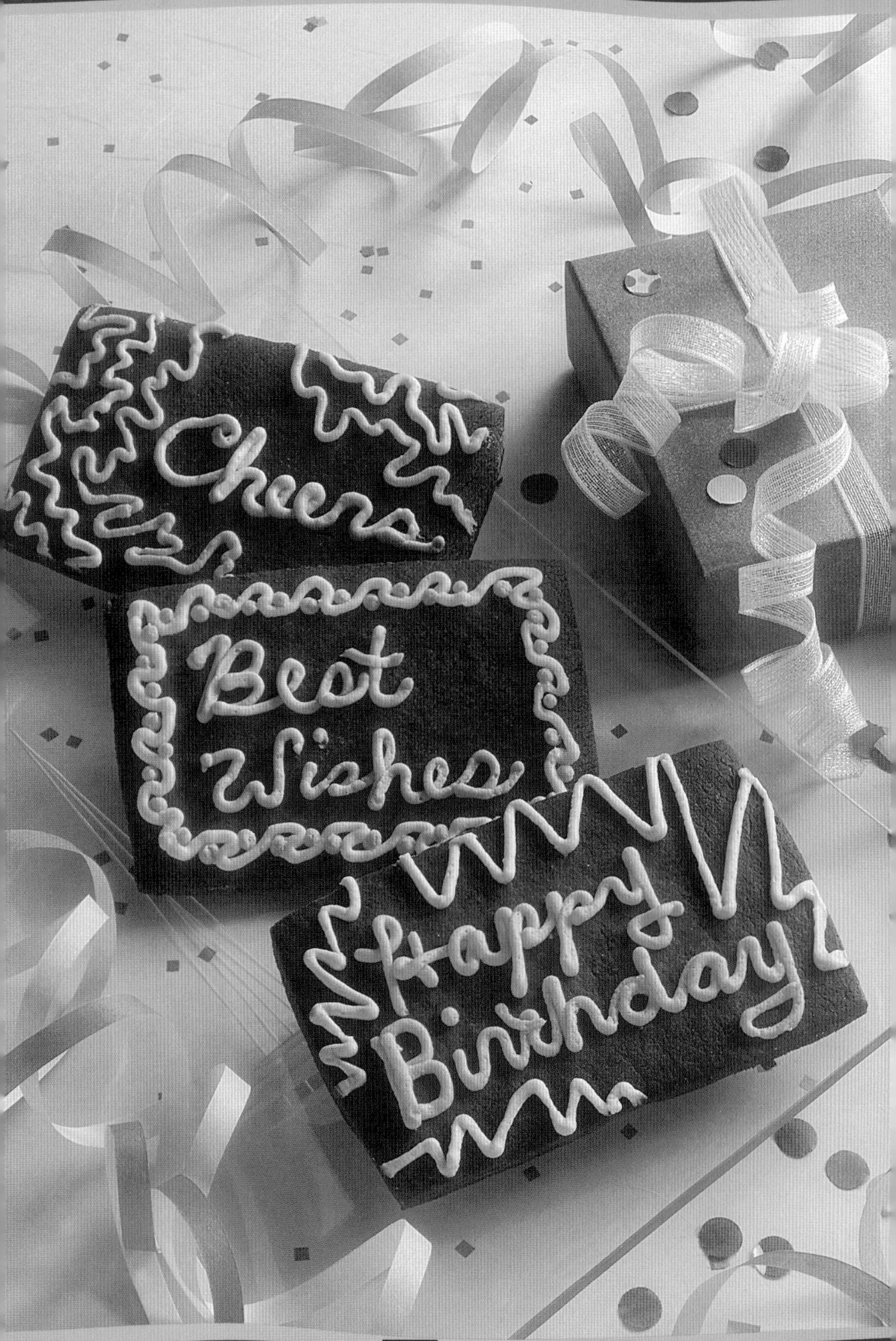
Cheers
Best Wishes
Happy Birthday

Greeting Card Cookies, continued

4. Prepare Decorative Frosting; spoon into pastry bag fitted with decorating tip. Pipe names or greetings onto cookies; decorate as desired.   *Makes about 12 cookies*

Decorative Frosting

3 cups powdered sugar
⅓ cup shortening
2 to 3 tablespoons milk
Food color (optional)

Beat sugar and shortening in small bowl; gradually add milk, beating until smooth and slightly thickened. Cover until ready to use. If desired, divide frosting into two or more bowls; tint each a different color with food color.

To use these cookies as gift tags, before baking, make a hole in one corner of the dough rectangle with a straw. Reshape the hole if necessary after baking. After decorating, tie the cookie on the gift with pretty ribbon.

Fudge-Filled Bars

**1 (14-ounce) can EAGLE BRAND® Sweetened Condensed
    Milk (NOT evaporated milk)**
1 (12-ounce) package semi-sweet chocolate chips
2 tablespoons butter or margarine
2 teaspoons vanilla extract
**2 (18-ounce) packages refrigerated cookie dough (oatmeal-
    chocolate chip, chocolate chip or sugar cookie dough)**

1. Preheat oven to 350°F. In heavy saucepan over medium heat, combine Eagle Brand, chips and butter; heat until chips melt, stirring often. Remove from heat; stir in vanilla. Cool 15 minutes.

2. Using floured hands, press 1½ packages of cookie dough into ungreased 15×10×1-inch baking pan. Pour cooled chocolate mixture evenly over dough. Crumble remaining dough over chocolate mixture.

3. Bake 25 to 30 minutes. Cool. Cut into bars. Store covered at room temperature.   *Makes 48 bars*

Prep Time: 20 minutes
Bake Time: 25 to 30 minutes

Hockey Sticks & Pucks

1 package (18 ounces) refrigerated sugar cookie dough
¾ cup all-purpose flour
24 miniature (¾-inch) chocolate-covered mint candies
Prepared icings

1. Grease cookie sheets. Remove dough from wrapper; place in large bowl. Let dough stand at room temperature 15 minutes.

2. Add flour to dough; knead until well blended. Divide dough into 24 pieces. Shape each piece into 6-inch-long rope. Place ropes on prepared cookie sheets; bend ropes about 1¾ inches from ends to form hockey stick shapes. Freeze 10 minutes.

3. Preheat oven to 350°F. Bake 8 to 10 minutes or until lightly browned. While cookies are still hot, place one mint on bottom part of each cookie for puck. Cool completely on cookie sheets.

4. Decorate with icings as desired. *Makes 2 dozen cookies*

Almond Alphabet Cookies

1 package (18 ounces) refrigerated sugar cookie dough
¼ cup all-purpose flour
1 to 1½ teaspoons almond extract
Assorted food colorings

1. Remove dough from wrapper; place in large bowl. Let dough stand at room temperature about 15 minutes.

2. Add flour and almond extract to dough; beat at medium speed of electric mixer until well blended. Divide dough into 3 equal pieces.

3. Combine each dough piece and desired food coloring in separate medium bowl; beat at medium speed of electric mixer until dough is evenly colored. Wrap doughs separately in plastic wrap; refrigerate 20 minutes.

4. Divide each color of dough into 9 equal pieces. Shape 1 piece of each color into 7-inch rope; sprinkle with additional flour to minimize sticking, if necessary. Braid 3 different colored ropes together, stretching gently to make 9- to 10-inch braid. Cut braid in half; shape each braid half into desired alphabet letter on ungreased cookie sheet. Repeat with remaining dough pieces to make 18 letters. Freeze letters at least 10 minutes.

5. Preheat oven to 350°F. Bake letters 9 to 11 minutes or until firm but not browned. Cool on cookie sheets 5 minutes. Remove to wire rack; cool completely.

Makes 1½ dozen cookies

Mud Cups

1 package (18 ounces) refrigerated sugar cookie dough
¼ cup unsweetened cocoa powder
3 containers (4 ounces each) chocolate pudding
1¼ cups chocolate sandwich cookie crumbs (about 15 cookies)
Gummy worms

1. Preheat oven to 350°F. Grease 18 (2½- or 2¾-inch) muffin pan cups.

2. Remove dough from wrapper; place in large bowl. Let dough stand at room temperature about 15 minutes.

3. Add cocoa to dough; beat at medium speed of electric mixer until well blended. Shape dough into 18 balls; press onto bottoms and up sides of prepared muffin cups.

4. Bake 12 to 14 minutes or until set. Remove from oven; gently press down center of each cookie with back of teaspoon. Cool in pan 10 minutes. Remove cups from pan; cool completely on wire rack.

5. Fill each cup with 1 to 2 tablespoons pudding; sprinkle with cookie crumbs. Garnish with gummy worms.

Makes 1½ dozen cookie cups

Mud Cups

Nothin' But Net

1 package (18 ounces) refrigerated sugar cookie dough
1¼ cups all-purpose flour
2 tablespoons powdered sugar
2 tablespoons fresh lemon juice
Orange, white and black decorating icings

1. Preheat oven to 350°F. Grease cookie sheets.

2. Remove dough from wrapper; place in large bowl. Let dough stand at room temperature about 15 minutes.

3. Add flour, powdered sugar and lemon juice to dough; beat until well blended. Divide dough in half. Wrap each half in plastic wrap; refrigerate at least 2 hours. Meanwhile, make pattern using diagram (see page 5).

4. Roll 1 dough half to ¼-inch thickness on lightly floured surface. Place pattern on dough. Cut around pattern with sharp knife; remove pattern from dough. Place cutouts 2 inches apart on prepared cookie sheets. Repeat with remaining dough.

5. Bake 13 to 15 minutes or until edges are lightly browned. Remove to wire rack; cool completely.

6. Decorate with icings as shown in photo.

Makes 1½ dozen cookies

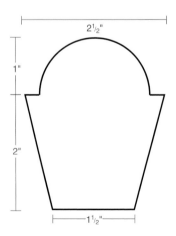

Nothin' But Net

Groovy Peace Signs

1 package (18 ounces) refrigerated sugar cookie dough
  Assorted colored hard candies, separated into colors and
    crushed

1. Preheat oven to 350°F. Line cookie sheets with foil; lightly grease foil.

2. Remove dough from wrapper, keeping in log shape. Cut dough log in half crosswise. Wrap 1 half in plastic wrap; refrigerate.

3. Cut remaining log into 12 equal slices using sharp knife. Pat into 2¼-inch rounds with floured hands. Place 2 inches apart on prepared cookie sheets.

4. Bake 6 to 7 minutes or until edges are lightly browned. While still warm, center 2-inch round cookie cutter over each cookie; gently press to make indentation. Loosen cookies from cookie sheet with metal spatula. Cut peace sign design with sharp knife; remove and discard scraps.

5. Fill cutout shapes with crushed candies. Do not overfill. Brush off any excess crushed candy with clean, dry pastry brush.

6. Return cookies to oven; bake 2 to 3 minutes or until candies are just melted. Remove foil and cookies to wire rack; cool completely. Repeat with remaining dough and candies.

Makes 2 dozen cookies

Tip: To crush hard candies, unwrap candies and separate into colors. Place each color in separate heavy resealable plastic food storage bag. Crush candies with rolling pin or hammer.

Building Blocks

1 package (18 ounces) refrigerated cookie dough, any flavor
Powdered Sugar Glaze (recipe follows)
Assorted food colorings
Assorted round fruit-flavored gummy candies (about ¼ inch in diameter)

1. Preheat oven to 350°F. Grease 13×9-inch baking pan.

2. Remove dough from wrapper; place in large bowl. Let dough stand at room temperature about 15 minutes.

3. Press dough evenly onto bottom of prepared pan. Score dough lengthwise and crosswise into 32 equal rectangles (about 1½×2¼ inches each) with sharp knife. Freeze 10 minutes.

4. Remove pan from freezer. Bake 10 minutes; remove from oven. Re-score partially baked cookies. Return pan to oven; bake 4 to 5 minutes or until edges are lightly browned and center is set. Cut through score marks to separate cookies. Cool in pan 10 minutes. Remove to wire rack; cool completely.

5. Prepare Powdered Sugar Glaze; divide into 3 or 4 bowls. Tint glaze with food colorings as desired.

6. Place wire rack over waxed paper. Spread glaze over tops and sides of cookies. Let stand about 5 minutes; place 6 gummy candies on each cookie. Let stand about 40 minutes or until completely set. *Makes about 2½ dozen cookies*

Powdered Sugar Glaze: Combine 2 cups powdered sugar and 6 tablespoons heavy cream in medium bowl; whisk until smooth. Add 1 to 2 tablespoons cream, 1 tablespoon at a time, to make medium-thick pourable glaze.

Snickerdoodle Batter Ups

1 package (18 ounces) refrigerated sugar cookie dough
1 teaspoon vanilla
¼ cup sugar
¼ teaspoon ground cinnamon
Chocolate and red decorating icings

1. Remove dough from wrapper; place in medium bowl. Let dough stand at room temperature about 15 minutes.

2. Add vanilla to dough; beat until well blended. Divide dough in half. Wrap each half in plastic wrap; refrigerate 1 hour.

3. Preheat oven to 350°F. For baseballs, roll 1 dough half to ¼-inch thickness on well-floured surface using well-floured rolling pin. Cut dough into circles using 2½-inch round cookie cutter. Reroll dough and scraps, if necessary, to make 12 circles.

4. Place cutouts on ungreased cookie sheets. Mix sugar and cinnamon in bowl; sprinkle over cutouts. Bake 8 to 10 minutes or until firm and edges are lightly browned. Cool on cookie sheets 3 minutes. Remove to wire rack; cool completely.

5. For bats, make pattern for bat using diagram (see page 5). (Or use 4-inch baseball bat-shaped cookie cutter.) Roll remaining dough half to ¼-inch thickness on well-floured surface using well-floured rolling pin. Place pattern on dough; cut around pattern with sharp knife. Repeat with remaining dough and scraps to make 12 bats.

6. Place cutouts on ungreased cookie sheets; sprinkle with cinnamon-sugar. Bake 8 to 10 minutes or until firm and edges are lightly browned. Cool on cookie sheets 3 minutes. Remove to wire rack; cool completely.

7. To decorate, pipe chocolate icing onto bats; pipe red icing onto balls for seams. *Makes 2 dozen cookies*

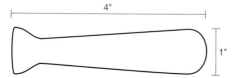

4"

1"

Snickerdoodle Batter Ups

Bulls-Eyes

1 package (18 ounces) refrigerated sugar cookie dough
Black and red food colorings

1. Remove dough from wrapper. Divide dough in half; place in separate medium bowls. Let dough stand at room temperature about 15 minutes.

2. Add black food coloring to dough in one bowl and red food coloring to dough in remaining bowl. Beat doughs separately until evenly colored. Wrap doughs separately in plastic wrap; refrigerate 1 hour.

3. Preheat oven to 350°F. Roll black dough on lightly floured waxed paper to ¼-inch thickness. Sprinkle dough with flour to minimize sticking, if necessary. Cut dough using 3-inch round cookie cutter; place cutouts 2 inches apart on ungreased cookie sheets. Repeat with red dough, cutting out same number of red circles as black circles.

4. Cut and remove circles from centers of 3-inch cutouts using 2-inch round cookie cutter. Place red 2-inch circles into centers of black 3-inch rings; place black 2-inch circles into centers of red 3-inch rings.

5. Cut and remove circles from centers of 2-inch cutouts using 1-inch round cookie cutter. Place red 1-inch circles into centers of black 2-inch rings; place black 1-inch circles into centers of red 2-inch rings.

6. Bake 8 to 11 minutes or until firm but not browned. Cool on cookie sheets 10 minutes. Remove to wire rack; cool completely.

Makes about 1½ dozen cookies

Tie-Dyed T-Shirts

1 package (18 ounces) refrigerated sugar cookie dough
6 tablespoons all-purpose flour, divided
Red, yellow and blue food colorings

1. Preheat oven to 350°F. Grease cookie sheets.

2. Remove dough from wrapper. Divide into 3 pieces; place in separate medium bowls. Let dough stand at room temperature about 15 minutes.

3. Add 2 tablespoons flour and red food coloring to dough in one bowl; beat at medium speed of electric mixer until well blended and evenly colored. Wrap in plastic wrap; refrigerate 20 minutes. Repeat with second dough piece, 2 tablespoons flour and yellow food coloring. Repeat with remaining dough piece, remaining 2 tablespoons flour and blue food coloring.

4. Divide each color in half. Press together half of yellow dough with half of red dough. Roll dough on lightly floured surface to ¼-inch thickness. Cut dough with 3-inch T-shirt-shaped cookie cutter or make pattern (see page 5). Place cutouts 2 inches apart on prepared cookie sheets. Repeat with remaining dough, pairing remaining yellow dough with half of blue dough and remaining red dough with remaining blue dough.

5. Bake 7 to 9 minutes or until firm but not browned. Cool completely on cookie sheets.

Makes about 1½ dozen cookies

ABC Blocks

2 recipes Sugar Cookie Dough (page 66)
Red food coloring

1. Prepare 2 recipes Sugar Cookie Dough as directed. Tint one recipe dough to desired shade of red with food coloring. Wrap doughs separately in plastic wrap; refrigerate 30 minutes.

2. Shape ⅔ red dough into 1½×1½×6-inch square log, pressing log on sides to flatten. Shape ⅔ plain dough into 1½×1½×6-inch square log, pressing log on sides to flatten.

3. Roll remaining ⅓ red dough into 6×7-inch rectangle on waxed paper. Place plain log in center of red rectangle. Fold red edges up and around plain log. Press gently on top and sides of dough so entire log is wrapped in red dough. Flatten log slightly to form square log. Wrap log in plastic wrap; refrigerate 1 hour. Repeat process with remaining ⅓ plain dough and red log.

4. Preheat oven to 350°F. Lightly grease cookie sheets. Cut each log into same number of ¼-inch-thick slices. Place slices 1 inch apart on prepared cookie sheets. Using 1½-inch cookie cutters, cut out letter shapes from blocks, making sure to cut same number of each letter from red and plain dough. Place red letters in plain blocks and plain letters in red blocks; press.

5. Bake 8 to 10 minutes. Cool on cookie sheets 1 minute. Remove to wire rack; cool completely.

Makes 2 dozen large cookies

continued on page 66

ABC Blocks

ABC Blocks, continued

Sugar Cookie Dough

2¼ cups all-purpose flour
¼ teaspoon salt
1 cup sugar
¾ cup (1½ sticks) unsalted butter, softened
1 egg
1 teaspoon vanilla
1 teaspoon almond extract

1. Combine flour and salt in medium bowl. Beat sugar and butter in large bowl at medium speed of electric mixer until fluffy.

2. Beat in egg, vanilla and almond extract. Gradually add flour mixture. Beat at low speed until well blended.

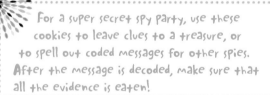

For a super secret spy party, use these cookies to leave clues to a treasure, or to spell out coded messages for other spies. After the message is decoded, make sure that all the evidence is eaten!

Delicious Dominos

6 squares (1 ounce each) semi-sweet chocolate
6 tablespoons butter
2 eggs
⅓ cup honey
1 teaspoon vanilla extract
½ cup all-purpose flour
½ teaspoon baking powder
Dash salt
1¼ cups "M&M's"® Chocolate Mini Baking Bits, divided
1 cup chocolate frosting
White Icing (recipe follows)

Preheat oven to 350°F. Line 8×8×2-inch baking pan with aluminum foil, leaving 1½-inch overhang on two opposite sides. Lightly grease foil; set pan aside. Place chocolate and butter in large microwave-safe bowl. Microwave at HIGH 1 minute; stir. Repeat as necessary until chocolate is completely melted, stirring at 10-second intervals. Let cool slightly. Stir in eggs, honey and vanilla. In medium bowl combine flour, baking powder and salt; add to chocolate mixture. Stir in 1 cup "M&M's"® Chocolate Mini Baking Bits. Spread mixture in prepared pan. Bake 20 to 25 minutes or just until center feels springy. Cool completely on wire rack. Lift brownies out of pan using foil. Spread brownies with chocolate frosting. Cut into 1¼×2-inch rectangles. Prepare White Icing. Spoon icing into small resealable plastic sandwich bag; seal bag. Cut tiny piece off one corner of bag (not more than ⅛ inch). Pipe icing in line across middle of each brownie bar. Decorate with remaining ¼ cup "M&M's"® Chocolate Mini Baking Bits to resemble dominos.   *Makes 2 dozen brownies*

White Icing: In medium bowl combine 1 cup powdered sugar, 1 tablespoon warm water and ¼ teaspoon vanilla extract until desired consistency.

Nutty Footballs

1 cup (2 sticks) butter, softened
½ cup sugar
1 egg
½ teaspoon vanilla
2 cups all-purpose flour
¼ cup unsweetened cocoa powder
1 cup finely chopped almonds
Prepared colored icings (optional)
Prepared white icing

1. Beat butter and sugar in large bowl at medium speed of electric mixer until creamy. Add egg and vanilla; beat until well blended. Combine flour and cocoa; gradually add to butter mixture, beating until well blended. Add almonds; beat until well blended. Shape dough into disc. Wrap in plastic wrap; refrigerate 30 minutes.

2. Preheat oven to 350°F. Lightly grease cookie sheets. Roll out dough on floured surface to ¼-inch thickness. Cut dough with 2½- to 3-inch football-shaped cookie cutter.* Place 2 inches apart on prepared cookie sheets.

3. Bake 10 to 12 minutes or until set. Cool on cookie sheets 1 to 2 minutes. Remove to wire rack; cool completely. Decorate with colored icings, if desired. Pipe white icing onto footballs to make laces. *Makes 2 dozen cookies*

*To make football shapes without a cookie cutter, shape 3 tablespoonfuls of dough into ovals. Place 3 inches apart on prepared cookie sheets. Flatten ovals to ¼-inch thickness; taper ends. Bake as directed.

Tic-Tac-Toe Cookies

¾ cup (1½ sticks) butter, softened
¾ cup granulated sugar
1 egg
1 teaspoon vanilla extract
2¼ cups all-purpose flour
½ teaspoon baking powder
¼ teaspoon salt
4 squares (1 ounce each) semi-sweet chocolate, melted
¼ cup powdered sugar
1 teaspoon water
½ cup "M&M's"® Chocolate Mini Baking Bits

In bowl cream butter and granulated sugar until light and fluffy; beat in egg and vanilla. In bowl mix flour, baking powder and salt; blend into creamed mixture. Reserve half of dough. Stir chocolate into remaining dough. Wrap; refrigerate doughs 30 minutes. Working with 1 dough at a time on lightly floured surface, roll or pat into 7×4½-inch rectangle. Cut dough into 9 (7×½-inch) strips. Repeat with remaining dough. Place 1 strip chocolate dough on sheet of plastic wrap. Place 1 strip vanilla dough next to chocolate dough. Place second strip of chocolate dough next to vanilla dough to make bottom layer. Prepare second row by stacking strips on first row, alternating vanilla dough over chocolate, and chocolate dough over vanilla. Repeat with third row to complete 1 bar. Repeat entire process with remaining dough strips, starting with vanilla dough, to complete second bar. Wrap both bars and refrigerate 1 hour. Preheat oven to 350°F. Grease cookie sheets. Cut bars crosswise into ¼-inch slices. Place 2 inches apart on prepared cookie sheets. Bake 10 to 12 minutes. Cool on cookie sheets 2 minutes; cool completely on wire racks. In bowl mix powdered sugar and water until smooth. Using icing to attach, decorate cookies with "M&M's"® Chocolate Mini Baking Bits to look like Tic-Tac-Toe games. *Makes 4 dozen cookies*

Tic-Tac-Toe Cookies

Ice Skates

½ cup (1 stick) butter, softened
1¼ cups honey
1 cup packed light brown sugar
1 egg, separated
5½ cups self-rising flour
1 teaspoon ground ginger
1 teaspoon ground cinnamon
½ cup milk
Prepared colored icings, sprinkles and small candy canes

1. Beat butter, honey, brown sugar and egg yolk in large bowl at medium speed of electric mixer until light and fluffy.

2. Combine flour, ginger and cinnamon in small bowl. Add alternately with milk to butter mixture; beat just until combined. Wrap in plastic wrap; refrigerate 30 minutes.

3. Preheat oven to 350°F. Grease cookie sheets.

4. Roll dough on lightly floured surface to ¼-inch thickness. Cut dough using 3½-inch boot-shaped cookie cutter or make pattern (see page 5). Place cutouts 2 inches apart on prepared cookie sheets.

5. Bake 8 to 10 minutes or until edges are lightly browned. Cool on cookie sheets 2 minutes. Remove to wire rack; cool completely.

6. Decorate cookies with colored icings and sprinkles to look like ice skates, attaching candy canes as skate blades.

Makes about 4 dozen cookies

Ice Skates

Journey to the land of Make Believe

Sparkling Magic Wands

1 package (18 ounces) refrigerated sugar cookie dough
48 pretzel sticks (2½ inches long)
   Prepared colored icings
   Colored sugar or edible glitter and gold dragees

1. Preheat oven to 350°F. Remove dough from wrapper.

2. Roll dough to ⅛-inch thickness on well-floured surface. Cut dough with 2-inch star-shaped cookie cutter. Place each star on top of 1 pretzel stick; press lightly to attach. Place on ungreased cookie sheet.

3. Bake 4 to 6 minutes or until edges are lightly browned. Carefully remove to wire rack; cool completely.

4. Spread icing on stars; sprinkle with colored sugar. Press dragees into points of stars. Let stand until set.

Makes 4 dozen cookies

Peanut Butter Aliens

1 package (18 ounces) refrigerated sugar cookie dough
½ cup creamy peanut butter
⅓ cup all-purpose flour
¼ cup powdered sugar
½ teaspoon vanilla
1 cup strawberry jam
Green decorating icing

1. Preheat oven to 350°F. Grease 2 cookie sheets. Remove dough from wrapper; place in large bowl. Let dough stand at room temperature about 15 minutes.

2. Add peanut butter, flour, powdered sugar and vanilla to dough; beat at medium speed of electric mixer until well blended. Divide dough in half; wrap 1 half in plastic wrap and refrigerate.

3. Roll remaining dough half to ¼-inch thickness on lightly floured surface. Cut into 14 (3-inch) rounds; pinch 1 side of each circle to make tear drop shape. Place cutouts 2 inches apart on prepared cookie sheets. Bake 12 to 14 minutes or until firm and lightly browned. Cool on cookie sheets 2 to 3 minutes. Remove to wire rack; cool completely.

4. Roll remaining dough to ¼-inch thickness on lightly floured surface. Cut into 14 (3-inch) rounds; pinch 1 side of each circle to make tear drop shape. Place cutouts 2 inches apart on prepared cookie sheets. Using sharp knife or mini cookie cutter, cut 2 oblong holes for eyes. Make small slit or third hole for mouth, if desired. Bake 12 to 14 minutes or until firm and lightly browned. Cool on cookie sheets 2 to 3 minutes. Remove to wire rack; cool completely.

5. Spread green icing on cookies with faces; let stand 10 minutes or until set. Spread about 1 tablespoon jam on each uncut cookie. To assemble, cover each jam-topped cookie with green face cookie.   *Makes 14 sandwich cookies*

Peanut Butter Aliens

Magic Lightning Bolts

1 package (18 ounces) refrigerated sugar cookie dough
1 cup prepared cream cheese frosting
Blue food coloring
Blue crackling candy or blue sugar

1. Grease cookie sheets. Remove dough from wrapper; divide in half. Wrap 1 dough half in plastic wrap and refrigerate.

2. Roll remaining dough half to ¼-inch thickness on well-floured surface. Cut into zigzag lightning shapes about ½-inch wide and 5½ inches long, dipping knife in flour as needed. Place cutouts 2 inches apart on prepared cookie sheets. Repeat with remaining dough. Refrigerate cutouts 1 hour.

3. Preheat oven to 350°F. Bake cookies 5 to 7 minutes or until firm and edges are lightly browned. Cool on cookie sheets 2 to 3 minutes. Remove to wire rack; cool completely.

4. Just before serving, combine cream cheese frosting and food coloring in medium bowl; stir until well blended. Spread about 1 tablespoon frosting on each cookie. Sprinkle crackling candy on each cookie.   *Makes about 2 dozen cookies*

Note: Do not frost and decorate cookies in advance. Crackling candy begins to lose its popping quality when it is exposed to air and moisture.

Tea Party Cookies

1 package (18 ounces) refrigerated sugar cookie dough
¼ cup all-purpose flour
1 teaspoon apple pie spice*
Almond Royal Icing (page 86)
Assorted food colorings, candy fruit slices and assorted decors and sprinkles

*Substitute ½ teaspoon ground cinnamon, ¼ teaspoon ground nutmeg and ⅛ teaspoon ground allspice or ground cloves for 1 teaspoon apple pie spice.

1. Preheat oven to 350°F. Grease 6 (3-inch) muffin pan cups. Remove dough from wrapper; place in large bowl. Let dough stand at room temperature about 15 minutes.

2. Add flour and apple pie spice to dough; beat until well blended. Divide dough in half. Wrap 1 half in plastic wrap; refrigerate until needed.

3. For cups, shape dough into 6 balls; press onto bottoms and up sides of muffin cups. Freeze 10 minutes.

4. Bake cups 8 minutes. Immediately press back of floured round measuring spoon against sides and bottoms of cups to reshape. Bake 5 to 7 minutes; reshape, if necessary. Cool in pan 3 minutes. Remove to wire rack; cool completely.

5. For saucers, shape remaining dough into 6 (3-inch) discs. Place 2 inches apart on ungreased cookie sheets. Bake 7 minutes or until edges are lightly browned. Press down centers. Cool on cookie sheets 3 minutes. Remove to wire rack; cool completely.

6. Prepare Almond Royal Icing; spread on insides of cups. Let stand until set. Keep remaining icing tightly covered.

7. Tint remaining icing desired colors. With icing, attach 1 fruit slice to each cup for handle. Decorate as desired. Let stand 30 minutes or until set. To serve, place teacup cookies on saucer cookies. *Makes 6 teacup and saucer cookies*

Smilin' Cookies

1 package (18 ounces) refrigerated sugar cookie dough
4 teaspoons finely grated lemon peel
Yellow food coloring and yellow crystal sugar
¼ cup semisweet or milk chocolate chips

1. Remove dough from wrapper; place in large bowl. Let dough stand at room temperature about 15 minutes.

2. Add lemon peel and food coloring to dough; beat at medium speed of electric mixer until well blended and evenly colored. Wrap dough in plastic wrap; freeze 30 minutes.

3. Preheat oven to 350°F. Shape dough into 32 balls. Place 2 inches apart on ungreased cookie sheets; flatten into 1¾-inch rounds. Sprinkle with yellow sugar.

4. Bake 9 to 11 minutes or until set. Cool on cookie sheets 2 minutes. Remove to wire rack; cool completely.

5. Place chocolate chips in small resealable plastic food storage bag; seal. Microwave at HIGH (100% power) 1 minute; knead bag lightly. Microwave at HIGH for additional 30-second intervals until chips are completely melted, kneading bag after each interval. Cut off tiny corner of bag. Pipe chocolate onto cookies for eyes and mouths. *Makes 32 cookies*

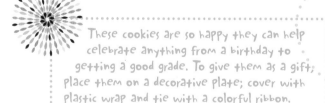

These cookies are so happy they can help celebrate anything from a birthday to getting a good grade. To give them as a gift, place them on a decorative plate; cover with plastic wrap and tie with a colorful ribbon.

Sour Spirals

1 package (18 ounces) refrigerated sugar cookie dough
2 tablespoons plus 1½ teaspoons blue raspberry-flavored gelatin
¼ teaspoon blue gel food coloring
2 tablespoons plus 1½ teaspoons strawberry-flavored gelatin
¼ teaspoon red gel food coloring

1. Remove dough from wrapper. Divide dough in half; place in separate medium bowls. Let dough stand about 15 minutes.

2. Add blue raspberry gelatin and blue food coloring to dough in one bowl. Add strawberry gelatin and red food coloring to dough in remaining bowl. Beat doughs separately at medium speed of electric mixer until well blended and evenly colored. Wrap doughs separately in plastic wrap; refrigerate 1 hour.

3. Roll blue dough to 6×10-inch rectangle on lightly floured waxed paper using lightly floured rolling pin. Repeat with red dough. Refrigerate both dough rectangles 10 minutes.

4. Flip blue dough onto red dough to cover. Remove waxed paper from blue dough. Starting at 10-inch side, roll up into tight log, removing waxed paper from red dough as it is rolled. Wrap in plastic wrap; freeze 30 minutes.

5. Preheat oven to 350°F. Grease cookie sheets. Cut log into ¼-inch slices. Place on prepared cookie sheets. Bake 8 to 10 minutes or until cookies are firm but not browned. Cool on cookie sheets 2 to 3 minutes. Remove to wire rack; cool completely.   *Makes about 2½ dozen cookies*

Cookie Necklaces

1 package (18 ounces) refrigerated sugar cookie dough
2 tablespoons all-purpose flour
1 tablespoon unsweetened Dutch process cocoa powder
Drinking straw
Almond Royal Icing (recipe follows) and colored sugars
Assorted food colorings and ¼-inch-wide curling ribbons
 in assorted colors, cut into lengths of 30 to 36 inches

1. Preheat oven to 350°F. Remove dough from wrapper; place in large bowl. Let dough stand at room temperature 15 minutes.

2. Add flour and cocoa to dough; beat until well blended. Divide dough into 4 equal pieces; wrap individually in plastic wrap and refrigerate 30 minutes.

3. Roll 1 dough piece on floured surface to ¼-inch thickness. Cut dough using 1- to 1½-inch cookie cutters. Place cutouts 2 inches apart on ungreased cookie sheets; make hole in center of each using straw. Repeat with remaining dough.

4. Bake 5 to 7 minutes or until firm but not browned. Make hole in center of each cutout again, if necessary. Cool on cookie sheets 2 minutes. Remove to wire rack; cool completely.

5. Prepare Almond Royal Icing; tint with food colorings as desired. Dip cookies into icings. Sprinkle with colored sugar. Let stand 40 minutes or until set.

6. Place 2 different color ribbons side by side; thread 9 or 10 cookies on each. Knot ribbons together at ends.

Makes about 100 miniature cookies
(enough for 10 necklaces)

Almond Royal Icing: Beat 2 egg whites (use only grade A, clean uncracked eggs) at high speed of electric mixer until foamy. Add 4 cups powdered sugar and ¾ teaspoon almond extract. Beat at low speed until moistened. Beat at high speed until icing is stiff; add additional powdered sugar if needed.

Cookie Necklace

Cowboy Macaroons

¾ Butter Flavor CRISCO® Stick or ¾ cup Butter Flavor CRISCO® all-vegetable shortening plus additional for greasing
1¼ cups firmly packed light brown sugar
1 egg
⅓ cup milk
1½ teaspoons vanilla
1½ cups quick oats, uncooked
1½ cups corn flakes
1 cup all-purpose flour
½ teaspoon baking soda
½ teaspoon salt
¼ teaspoon cinnamon
1 cup coarsely chopped walnuts
¾ cup finely chopped pecans
¾ cup flake coconut
⅓ cup maraschino cherries, cut into quarters (optional)

1. Heat oven to 375°F. Grease baking sheets. Place sheets of foil on countertop for cooling cookies.

2. Combine ¾ cup shortening, brown sugar, egg, milk and vanilla in large bowl. Beat at medium speed of electric mixer until well blended.

3. Combine oats, corn flakes, flour, baking soda, salt and cinnamon. Mix into creamed mixture at low speed just until blended. Stir in nuts, coconut and cherries.

4. Form dough into 1-inch balls. Place 2 inches apart onto prepared baking sheets.

5. Bake one baking sheet at a time at 375°F for 10 to 12 minutes, or until lightly browned. *Do not overbake.* Cool 2 minutes on baking sheet. Remove cookies to foil to cool completely. *Makes about 3 dozen cookies*

Happy Face Oatmeal Monsters

1½ cups all-purpose flour
1 teaspoon baking soda
½ teaspoon salt
1 cup (2 sticks) butter, softened
1 cup firmly packed light brown sugar
2 eggs
1 teaspoon vanilla
2 cups uncooked quick oats
Granulated sugar
28 candy-coated chocolate pieces or large chocolate chips
Cinnamon red hot candies or red licorice strings
Prepared colored frosting and shredded coconut
(optional)

1. Preheat oven to 350°F.

2. Combine flour, baking soda and salt in small bowl; set aside. Beat butter and brown sugar in large bowl at medium speed of electric mixer until light and fluffy. Beat in eggs, 1 at a time, until well blended. Beat in vanilla. Gradually beat in flour mixture at low speed until blended. Stir in oats.

3. Drop dough by level ¼ cupfuls 3 inches apart onto ungreased cookie sheets. Flatten dough with bottom of glass that has been dipped in granulated sugar until dough is 2 inches in diameter. Press chocolate pieces into cookies for eyes; use cinnamon candies or licorice for mouth.

4. Bake 12 to 14 minutes or until cookies are set and edges are golden brown. Cool on cookie sheets 2 minutes. Remove to wire rack; cool completely.

5. Decorate cookies with frosting and coconut for hair, if desired.   *Makes about 14 (4-inch) cookies*

Flying Saucers

1 package (18 ounces) refrigerated sugar cookie dough in
squares or rounds (20 count)
20 peppermint patties (1¼-inch diameter), unwrapped
2 egg yolks, lightly beaten
Assorted food colorings
20 round gummy candies

1. Preheat oven to 350°F. Grease cookie sheets.

2. Remove dough from wrapper; let stand at room temperature about 15 minutes.

3. Flatten each dough square or round to ¼-inch thickness. Place peppermint patty in center; press dough up and around patty to cover completely. Place on prepared cookie sheet; repeat with remaining dough and patties.

4. Divide egg yolks among 3 small bowls. Add different food coloring to each; beat lightly. Paint yolk mixtures onto unbaked cookies as desired using small, clean craft paintbrushes. Press gummy candy into center of each cookie.

5. Bake 10 minutes or until edges are lightly browned. Cool on cookie sheets 5 minutes. Remove to wire rack; cool completely.

Makes 20 cookies

Flying Saucers

Goofy Gus

1 package (18 ounces) refrigerated sugar cookie dough
1 egg yolk
¼ teaspoon water
Red food coloring
Prepared white frosting
10 packages (2 cakes each) coconut and marshmallow
covered, snowball-shaped cakes
Assorted candies and tinted shredded coconut

1. Preheat oven to 350°F. Remove dough from wrapper.

2. Roll dough to ⅛-inch thickness on well-floured surface. Cut with 2¼-inch foot-shaped cookie cutter. Place cutouts 2 inches apart on ungreased cookie sheets, turning half of cookies over to make both left and right feet.

3. Combine egg yolk, water and food coloring in small bowl; stir until well blended. Using small, clean craft paintbrush, paint egg yolk mixture on feet to make toenails.

4. Bake 5 to 8 minutes or until golden brown. Remove to wire rack; cool completely.

5. Using small amount of frosting, attach 1 right and 1 left foot to each snowball cake. Decorate with assorted candies and coconut as desired.   *Makes 20 desserts*

Goofy Gus

Chocolate Stars

1 package (18 ounces) refrigerated sugar cookie dough in squares or rounds (20 count)
1 tablespoon unsweetened Dutch process cocoa powder
½ cup slivered almonds, toasted* and finely chopped

*To toast almonds, spread in single layer on baking sheet. Bake in preheated 350°F oven 7 to 10 minutes or until golden brown, stirring frequently.

1. Preheat oven to 350°F. Lightly grease cookie sheets.

2. Remove dough from wrapper; let stand at room temperature about 15 minutes.

3. Combine 3 dough squares or rounds and cocoa in medium bowl; beat at medium speed of electric mixer until well blended. Wrap in plastic wrap; refrigerate 20 minutes.

4. Roll chocolate dough on lightly floured surface to ⅛-inch thickness. Cut dough with 1½-inch star cookie cutter; place cutouts 2 inches apart on ungreased cookie sheets. Reroll and cut dough scraps, if necessary to make 18 stars. Bake stars 3 to 5 minutes or until firm. Cool on cookie sheets 2 minutes. Remove to wire rack; cool completely.

5. Place almonds in shallow bowl. Shape remaining dough squares or rounds into balls; roll in nuts to cover evenly. Place 2 inches apart on prepared cookie sheets. Bake 10 to 12 minutes or until edges are firm and centers are slightly soft. Remove from oven; press one chocolate star cookie into center of each round cookie. Cool on cookie sheets 2 minutes. Remove to wire rack; cool completely.

Makes about 1½ dozen cookies

Moon Rocks

1 package (18 ounces) refrigerated sugar cookie dough
1 cup uncooked quick oats
¾ cup butterscotch chips
¾ cup yogurt-covered raisins

1. Preheat oven to 350°F. Lightly grease cookie sheets.

2. Remove dough from wrapper; place in large bowl. Let dough stand at room temperature about 15 minutes.

3. Add oats, butterscotch chips and raisins to dough; beat at medium speed of electric mixer until well blended. Drop dough by rounded teaspoonfuls 2 inches apart onto prepared cookie sheets.

4. Bake 9 to 11 minutes or until set. Cool on cookie sheets 1 minute. Remove to wire rack; cool completely.

Makes 3 dozen cookies

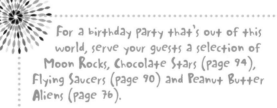

For a birthday party that's out of this world, serve your guests a selection of Moon Rocks, Chocolate Stars (page 94), Flying Saucers (page 90) and Peanut Butter Aliens (page 76).

Moon Rocks

Whirligigs

1 package (18 ounces) refrigerated sugar cookie dough
¼ cup all-purpose flour
½ teaspoon *each* banana and strawberry extract (optional)
Red and yellow food colorings
Colored sugar (optional)
12 (8-inch) lollipop sticks or wooden popsicle sticks*

*Lollipop sticks and popsicle sticks are available at crafts stores and where cake decorating supplies are sold.

1. Preheat oven to 350°F. Grease cookie sheets.

2. Remove dough from wrapper; place in medium bowl. Let dough stand at room temperature about 15 minutes.

3. Add flour to dough; beat at medium speed of electric mixer until well blended. Divide dough in half; place in separate bowls. Add banana extract, if desired, and yellow food coloring to dough in one bowl. Add strawberry extract, if desired, and red food coloring to dough in remaining bowl. Beat doughs separately at medium speed of electric mixer until well blended and evenly colored. Wrap doughs separately in plastic wrap; freeze dough 30 minutes.

4. Shape red dough into rope about 18 inches long on lightly floured surface. Repeat with yellow dough. Twist ropes together. Divide rope into 3 equal pieces. Working with one piece at a time, shape dough into rope about 20 inches long. Cut into 4 equal pieces. Coil each piece into circle; place 2 inches apart on prepared cookie sheets. (Make sure to leave room for lollipop sticks.) Sprinkle cookies with colored sugar, if desired. Refrigerate about 15 minutes. Repeat with remaining dough.

5. Carefully poke lollipop stick into edge of each cookie. Bake 12 to 15 minutes or until edges are lightly browned. Cool completely on cookie sheets.

Makes 1 dozen (3-inch) cookies

Whirligigs

Lone Star Peanut Butter Cutouts

¼ cup smooth peanut butter
¼ cup granulated sugar
3 tablespoons butter or margarine, softened
1¼ cups buttermilk baking mix
2 tablespoons water
½ teaspoon ground cinnamon
⅔ cup dry-roasted peanut halves
½ cup semi-sweet chocolate chips

In a large bowl, stir together peanut butter, sugar and butter or margarine until smooth. Stir in baking mix, water and cinnamon until well blended. Shape dough into a ball. Wrap dough with plastic wrap and chill about 1 hour or until firm. Cut dough in half. Roll each piece ⅛ inch thick on a lightly floured surface. Cut dough into stars with a cookie cutter. Transfer cutouts to ungreased cookie sheets. Press a few roasted peanut halves into the center of each cookie. Bake in a 375°F oven for 8 to 10 minutes, or until golden brown around the edges. With a spatula, transfer cookies to a cooling rack.

Melt chocolate chips in microwave on high power for 1 to 1½ minutes. Stir until smooth. Drizzle melted chocolate over each cookie. Refrigerate until chocolate is set. Store cookies in an airtight container. *Makes about 2 dozen cookies*

Favorite recipe from **Texas Peanut Producers Board**

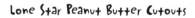

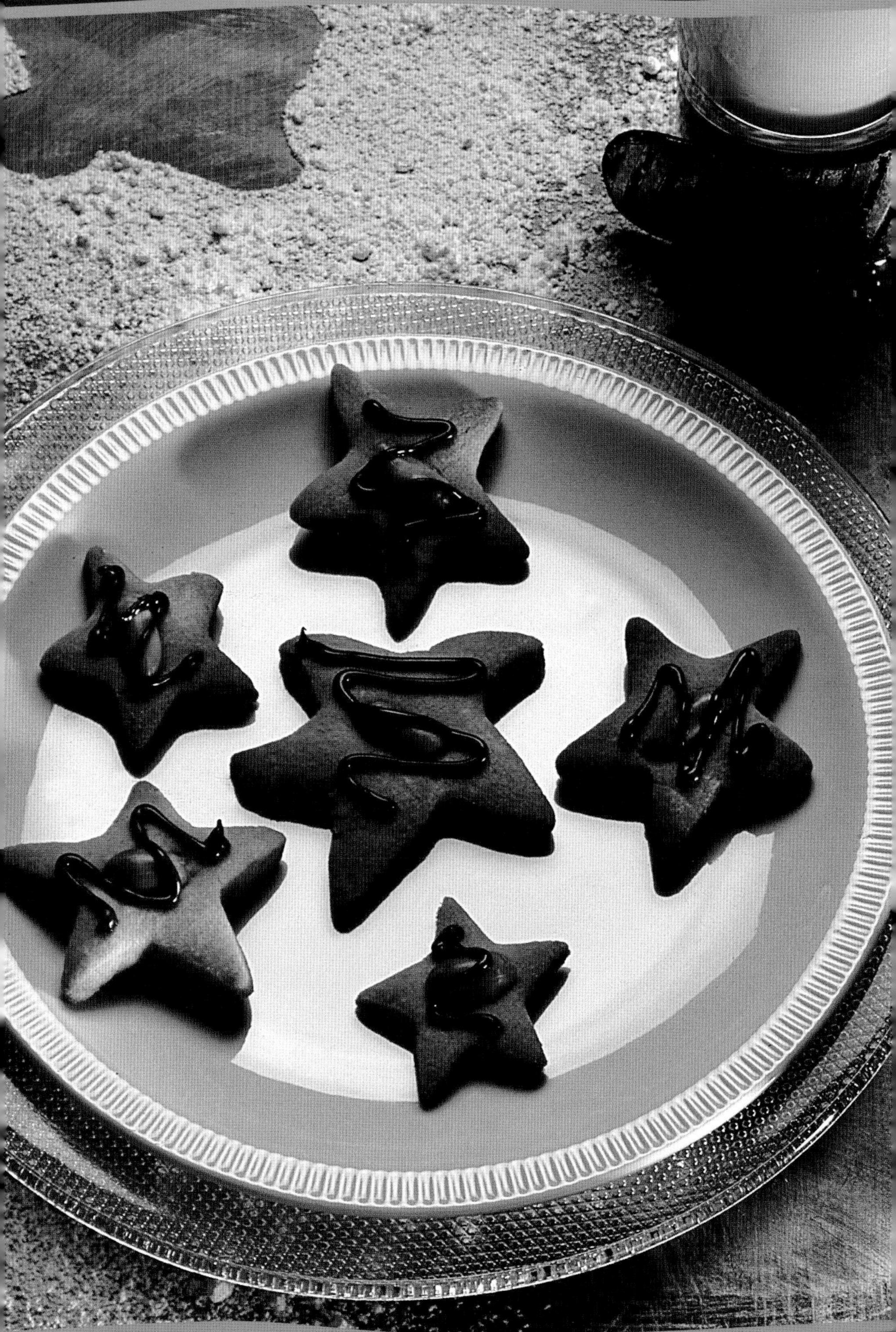

Coconut Craters

1 package (18 ounces) refrigerated chocolate chip cookie
   dough
¼ cup packed light brown sugar
2 tablespoons milk
1 tablespoon butter or margarine, melted
1 cup flaked coconut
½ cup chocolate-covered toffee baking pieces

1. Preheat oven to 350°F. Line 36 (1¾-inch) mini muffin pan
cups with paper baking cups.

2. Remove dough from wrapper. Shape dough into 36 balls;
press onto bottoms and up sides of muffin cups. Bake 9 to
11 minutes or until golden brown.

3. Meanwhile, combine brown sugar, milk and butter in
medium bowl. Stir in coconut and toffee pieces. Gently press
down center of each cookie with back of teaspoon. Spoon
1 rounded teaspoon toffee mixture into each cup. Bake 2 to
4 minutes or until golden. Cool in pan 10 minutes. Remove to
wire rack; cool completely.   *Makes 3 dozen cookies*

Masquerade Party Cookies

**1 package (18 ounces) refrigerated chocolate chip cookie
   dough**
¼ cup all-purpose flour
Colored nonpareils or sprinkles
Prepared black frosting
Red string licorice, cut into 5-inch lengths

1. Preheat oven to 350°F. Lightly grease cookie sheets. Remove dough from wrapper; place in large bowl. Let dough stand at room temperature about 15 minutes.

2. Add flour to dough; beat at medium speed of electric mixer until well blended.

3. Shape dough into 20 (3-inch long) ovals; roll in nonpareils. Place 2 inches apart on prepared cookie sheets; flatten slightly. Pinch ovals in at centers to create mask shapes. Decorate with additional nonpareils.

4. Bake 8 to 10 minutes or until edges are lightly browned. Make oval indentations for eyes with back of spoon. Reshape at centers, if necessary. Cool completely on cookie sheets.

5. Spread eye area with black frosting. Attach licorice piece to each side of mask with additional frosting. Let stand until frosting is set.   *Makes 20 cookies*

Masquerade Party Cookies

Snowcapped Mountains

1 package (18 ounces) refrigerated chocolate chip and
   walnut cookie dough in squares or rounds (20 count)
2 cups cornflakes
½ cup all-purpose flour
24 milk chocolate candy kisses, unwrapped
¼ cup powdered sugar

1. Preheat oven to 350°F. Grease cookie sheets.

2. Remove dough from wrapper; place in large bowl. Let dough stand at room temperature about 15 minutes.

3. Add cornflakes and flour to dough; beat at medium speed of electric mixer until well blended. Shape about 2 tablespoons dough into ball. Press 1 candy into center; wrap dough up and around candy to cover completely. Place on prepared cookie sheets. Repeat with remaining dough and candies.

4. Bake 8 to 10 minutes or until lightly browned. Cool on cookie sheets 5 minutes. Remove to wire rack; cool completely.

5. Sprinkle cooled cookies with powdered sugar.

Makes 2 dozen cookies

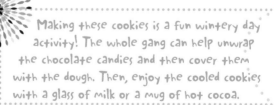

Making these cookies is a fun wintery day activity! The whole gang can help unwrap the chocolate candies and then cover them with the dough. Then, enjoy the cooled cookies with a glass of milk or a mug of hot cocoa.

Adventures in the Animal Kingdom

Animal Pawprints

1 package (18 ounces) refrigerated sugar cookie dough
¼ cup unsweetened cocoa powder
Regular-sized and mini peanut butter chips

1. Preheat oven to 350°F. Grease cookie sheets.

2. Remove dough from wrapper; place in large bowl. Let dough stand at room temperature about 15 minutes.

3. Add cocoa to dough; beat at medium speed of electric mixer until well blended. For each cookie, shape 1 (1-inch) ball and 4 smaller balls. Place large ball on prepared cookie sheet; place small balls on one side of large ball.

4. Bake 12 to 14 minutes or until cookies are set and no longer shiny. Remove from oven; immediately place regular-sized peanut butter chip on first "toe" and place mini peanut butter chips on remaining "toes" of each cookie. Remove to wire rack; cool completely. *Makes 1½ dozen cookies*

Fido's Favorite Things

1 package (18 ounces) refrigerated oatmeal raisin cookie dough in squares or rounds (12 count)
Prepared colored icings
Colored sugars
Coarsely chopped pretzel sticks

1. Preheat oven to 350°F. Lightly grease cookie sheets.

2. Remove dough from wrapper; let stand at room temperature about 15 minutes.

3. For bone, shape dough square or round into 3½-inch-long rectangle with floured hands. Make indentations in ends to resemble dog bone*. For food dish, pat dough square or round into 2-inch square; taper top to 1¾ inches and flare bottom to 3 inches. For fire hydrant, shape dough square or round into 2×1-inch fire hydrant shape*. Place dough shapes 2 inches apart on prepared cookie sheets.

4. Bake 13 to 15 minutes or until edges are lightly browned. Cool on cookie sheets 5 minutes. Remove to wire rack; cool completely.

5. Decorate with icings, sugars and pretzels as desired.

Makes 1 dozen cookies

*Or flatten dough with floured hands or rolling pin and cut with 2- to 3-inch cookie cutters.

Fido's Favorite Things

Dino-Mite Dinosaurs

1 cup (2 sticks) butter, softened
1¼ cups granulated sugar
1 egg
2 squares (1 ounce each) semi-sweet chocolate, melted
½ teaspoon vanilla extract
2⅓ cups all-purpose flour
1 teaspoon baking powder
¼ teaspoon salt
1 cup white frosting
Assorted food colorings
1 cup "M&M's"® Chocolate Mini Baking Bits

In large bowl cream butter and sugar until light and fluffy; beat in egg, chocolate and vanilla. In medium bowl combine flour, baking powder and salt; add to creamed mixture. Wrap and refrigerate dough 2 to 3 hours. Preheat oven to 350°F. Working with half the dough at a time on lightly floured surface, roll to ¼-inch thickness. Cut into dinosaur shapes using 4-inch cookie cutters. Place about 2 inches apart on ungreased cookie sheets. Bake 10 to 12 minutes. Cool 2 minutes on cookie sheets; cool completely on wire racks. Tint frosting desired colors. Frost cookies and decorate with "M&M's"® Chocolate Mini Baking Bits. Store in tightly covered container. *Makes 2 dozen cookies*

Luscious Lions

Manes
   1 package (18 ounces) refrigerated sugar cookie dough
   ¼ cup all-purpose flour
   2 tablespoons powdered sugar
   Grated peel of 1 large orange
   ¼ teaspoon yellow gel food coloring
   ¼ teaspoon red gel food coloring

Faces
   ½ (18-ounce) package refrigerated sugar cookie dough*
   2 tablespoons all-purpose flour
   1 tablespoon powdered sugar
   Grated peel of 1 lemon
   ¼ teaspoon yellow gel food coloring
   Mini candy-coated chocolate pieces
   Prepared white icing
   Assorted decors
   Prepared chocolate icing or melted chocolate

*Save remaining ½ package of dough for another use.

1. Grease 2 cookie sheets. For manes, remove 1 package dough from wrapper; place in large bowl. Let dough stand at room temperature about 15 minutes.

2. Add flour, powdered sugar, orange peel, yellow food coloring and red food coloring to dough; beat at medium speed of electric mixer until well blended and evenly colored. Shape into 24 large balls. Place 12 balls on each cookie sheet. Flatten balls into circles about 2¾ inches in diameter. Cut each circle with fluted 2½-inch round cookie cutter. Remove scraps and discard. Refrigerate 30 minutes.

continued on page 116

Luscious Lions, continued

3. Preheat oven to 350°F. Bake manes 12 to 14 minutes or until edges are lightly browned. Cool on cookie sheets 2 to 3 minutes. Remove to wire rack; cool completely.

4. For faces, remove ½ package of dough from wrapper; place in medium bowl. Let dough stand at room temperature about 15 minutes.

5. Add flour, powdered sugar, lemon peel and yellow food coloring to dough; beat at medium speed of electric mixer until well blended and evenly colored. Shape into 24 balls. Place on prepared cookie sheets. Flatten balls to slightly larger than 1½ inches in diameter. Cut into circles using smooth 1½-inch round cookie cutter. Remove scraps; shape into balls for ears. Attach 2 ears to each face. Place 2 candy pieces in center of each ear and place 1 candy piece for nose.

6. Bake 14 minutes or until edges are lightly browned. Cool on cookie sheets 2 to 3 minutes. Remove to wire rack; cool completely.

7. To assemble lions attach faces to manes with icing. Pipe white icing onto faces and press decors into icing for eyes. Pipe chocolate icing onto faces for whiskers.

Makes 2 dozen cookies

Use the remaining half package of refrigerated sugar cookie dough to make lioness cookies! Simply follow the recipe and directions for making the lion faces, but after baking, do not attach them to manes.

Go Fish

½ cup (1 stick) butter, softened
¾ cup granulated sugar
¼ cup firmly packed light brown sugar
1 egg
1 egg white
½ teaspoon vanilla extract
2 cups all-purpose flour
1¼ teaspoons ground cinnamon
1 teaspoon baking powder
1 cup white frosting
Assorted food colorings
1 cup "M&M's"® Chocolate Mini Baking Bits

In large bowl cream butter and sugars until light and fluffy; beat in egg, egg white and vanilla. In medium bowl combine flour, cinnamon and baking powder; add to creamed mixture. Wrap and refrigerate dough 2 to 3 hours. Preheat oven to 325°F. Working with half the dough at a time on lightly floured surface, roll to ¼-inch thickness. Cut into fish shapes using 3-inch cookie cutters. Place about 2 inches apart on ungreased cookie sheets. Bake 10 to 12 minutes. Cool 2 minutes on cookie sheets; cool completely on wire racks. Tint frosting desired colors. Frost cookies and decorate with "M&M's"® Chocolate Mini Baking Bits. Store in tightly covered container.   *Makes 2½ dozen cookies*

Chocolate Tortoises

1 package (18 ounces) refrigerated sugar cookie dough
⅓ cup unsweetened cocoa powder
1 tablespoon powdered sugar
½ teaspoon vanilla
30 caramels, unwrapped
   Pecan halves
½ cup (3 ounces) semisweet chocolate chips
   Silver dragees or decors

1. Preheat oven to 350°F. Grease mini (1¾-inch) muffin pan cups. Remove dough from wrapper; place in large bowl. Let dough stand at room temperature about 15 minutes.

2. Add cocoa, powdered sugar and vanilla to dough; beat at medium speed of electric mixer until well blended.

3. Shape dough into 30 balls; press onto bottoms and up sides of muffin cups. Bake 10 minutes. Press 1 caramel into each chocolate cup. Return to oven 2 to 3 minutes or until caramels are soft. Working quickly, press 5 pecans into caramel for legs and head. Let cool in pan 5 minutes. Remove to wire rack; cool completely.

4. Place wire rack over waxed paper. Place chocolate chips in small microwavable bowl. Microwave at HIGH 1 to 1½ minutes. Stir after 1 minute and at 30-second intervals after first minute until chips are melted and smooth. Attach 2 silver dragees to head with chocolate for eyes. Drizzle remaining chocolate over tops of tortoises as desired. Let stand until chocolate is completely set.

Makes 2½ dozen cookies

Chocolate Tortoises

Peanut Butter Bears

2 cups uncooked quick oats
2 cups all-purpose flour
1 tablespoon baking powder
1 cup granulated sugar
¾ cup (1½ sticks) butter, softened
½ cup packed brown sugar
½ cup creamy peanut butter
½ cup cholesterol-free egg substitute *or* 2 eggs
1 teaspoon vanilla
3 tablespoons miniature chocolate chips

1. Combine oats, flour and baking powder in medium bowl; set aside.

2. Combine granulated sugar, butter, brown sugar and peanut butter in large bowl; beat at medium-high speed of electric mixer until well blended. Add egg substitute and vanilla; beat until light and fluffy. Add oat mixture. Beat at low speed until blended. Wrap in plastic wrap; refrigerate 1 to 2 hours or until firm.

3. Preheat oven to 375°F.

4. For each bear, shape 1 (1-inch) ball for body and 1 (¾-inch) ball for head. Place body and head together on prepared cookie sheet; flatten slightly. Make 7 small balls for ears, arms, legs and mouth. Place on bear body and head. Place 2 chocolate chips on each head for eyes; place 1 chocolate chip on each body for belly-button.

5. Bake 9 to 11 minutes or until edges are lightly browned. Cool 1 minute on cookie sheets. Remove to wire rack; cool completely. *Makes 4 dozen cookies*

Peanut Butter Bear

Spiky Hedgehogs

1 package (18 ounces) refrigerated chocolate chip cookie
dough with caramel filling in squares or rounds (20 count)
½ cup uncooked quick or old-fashioned oats
½ cup all-purpose flour
2½ packages (1.5 ounces each) chocolate-covered crisp wafer
candy bars, separated into sticks
⅔ cup creamy peanut butter
2 tablespoons butter or margarine
1 cup powdered sugar
½ teaspoon vanilla
2 to 3 tablespoons milk
1 cup toasted coconut
Mini chocolate chips

1. Grease cookie sheets. Remove dough from wrapper; place in large bowl. Let dough stand at room temperature 15 minutes.

2. Add oats and flour to dough; beat until well blended.

3. Cut candy sticks in half crosswise to make 20 pieces. Divide dough into 20 pieces. Wrap dough pieces around candy pieces, completely covering tops and sides. Place 2 inches apart on prepared cookie sheets; pinch 1 end of dough to make pointy. Freeze 10 minutes or until firm.

4. Preheat oven to 350°F. Bake cookies 10 to 12 minutes or until firm and edges are lightly browned. Cool on cookie sheets 2 minutes. Remove to wire rack; cool completely.

5. Beat peanut butter and butter until well blended. Stir in powdered sugar and vanilla. Add milk by tablespoons until of desired frosting consistency. Reserve 1 tablespoon frosting.

6. Frost cookie tops and sides with remaining frosting, leaving pointed ends unfrosted. Place coconut in bowl. Dip frosted ends of cookies into coconut to cover. Using reserved frosting, attach chocolate chips for eyes and noses on pointed ends of each cookie. *Makes 20 cookies*

Spiky Hedgehogs

Sugar Cookie Fruit Tartlets

1 package (18 ounces) refrigerated sugar cookie dough
1 package (8 ounces) fat-free cream cheese, softened
¼ cup orange marmalade
2 teaspoons sugar
1 teaspoon vanilla
Assorted fresh and/or canned fruit

1. Preheat oven to 375°F. Lightly grease cookie sheets.

2. Remove dough from wrapper, keeping in log shape. Cut dough into 16 slices. Place 2 inches apart on prepared cookie sheets. Bake 10 to 14 minutes or until edges are lightly browned. Cool on cookie sheets 1 minute. Remove to wire rack; cool completely.

3. Meanwhile for frosting, beat cream cheese, marmalade, sugar and vanilla in medium bowl at high speed of electric mixer until well blended. Cover with plastic wrap; refrigerate.

4. Spread frosting on cooled cookies. Arrange fruit on top of frosting to make butterflies, flowers or other designs as desired. Serve immediately or store in tightly covered container in refrigerator. *Makes 16 cookies*

It's easy to change the flavor of these fruity cookies just by substituting your favorite jam for the orange marmalade. For the best results, make sure that canned fruit is drained well before arranging on the cookies.

Sugar Cookie Fruit Tartlets

Octo-Cookies

1 package (18 ounces) refrigerated chocolate chip cookie dough
¼ cup all-purpose flour
10 whole almonds (or 10 walnut or pecan halves)
Powdered Sugar Glaze (page 128)
Assorted food colorings
Prepared colored icings and candies

1. Preheat oven to 350°F. Grease 10 (1¾-inch) mini muffin pan cups. Remove dough from wrapper; place in large bowl. Let dough stand at room temperature about 15 minutes.

2. Add flour to dough; beat at medium speed of electric mixer until well blended. Reserve ⅓ of dough. Wrap remaining ⅔ of dough in plastic wrap; refrigerate.

3. For heads, divide reserved ⅓ dough into 10 equal pieces. Place almond in center of each piece; shape into balls, covering nut completely. Place balls in prepared muffin cups. Freeze 10 minutes. Bake 10 minutes or just until firm. Gently loosen cookies around edges with tip of small knife or metal spatula. Cool in pan 10 minutes. Remove to wire rack; cool completely.

4. For legs, divide remaining dough into 10 equal portions. Divide each portion into 8 pieces; shape each piece into ropes of varying lengths from 1½ to 2 inches long. Shape tips at one end to a point. Arrange 8 legs with thicker end of legs touching in center and pointed ends about ¼ inch away from each other at outside of circular shape. Bake 6 to 8 minutes or just until legs are firm. Cool completely on cookie sheets.

continued on page 128

Octo-Cookies

Octo-Cookies, continued

5. Place wire racks over waxed paper. Carefully transfer legs to wire racks. Prepare Powdered Sugar Glaze; tint glaze with food colorings as desired.

6. Attach heads to legs using glaze; let stand 15 minutes or until set. Spread remaining glaze over cookies. Let stand about 40 minutes or until completely set.

7. Outline legs and decorate faces with icings and candies as desired.
Makes 10 large cookies

Powdered Sugar Glaze

2 cups powdered sugar
7 to 9 tablespoons heavy cream, divided

1. Combine powdered sugar and 6 tablespoons cream in medium bowl; whisk until smooth.

2. Add enough remaining cream, 1 tablespoon at a time, to make medium-thick pourable glaze.

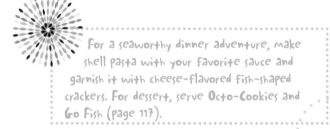

For a seaworthy dinner adventure, make shell pasta with your favorite sauce and garnish it with cheese-flavored fish-shaped crackers. For dessert, serve Octo-Cookies and Go Fish (page 117).

Monkey Bars

3 cups miniature marshmallows
½ cup honey
⅓ cup butter
¼ cup peanut butter
2 teaspoons vanilla
¼ teaspoon salt
4 cups crispy rice cereal
2 cups rolled oats, uncooked
½ cup flaked coconut
¼ cup peanuts

Combine marshmallows, honey, butter, peanut butter, vanilla and salt in medium saucepan. Melt marshmallow mixture over low heat, stirring constantly. Combine rice cereal, oats, coconut and peanuts in 13×9×2-inch baking pan. Pour marshmallow mixture over dry ingredients. Mix until thoroughly coated. Press mixture firmly into pan. Cool completely before cutting. *Makes 2 dozen bars*

Microwave Directions: Microwave marshmallows, honey, butter, peanut butter, vanilla and salt in 2-quart microwave-safe bowl on HIGH 2½ to 3 minutes. Continue as directed above.

Favorite recipe from **National Honey Board**

Czech Bear Paws

4 cups ground toasted hazelnuts
2 cups all-purpose flour
1 tablespoon unsweetened cocoa powder
1 teaspoon ground cinnamon
½ teaspoon ground nutmeg
¼ teaspoon salt
1 cup (2 sticks) plus 3 teaspoons butter, softened, divided
1 cup powdered sugar
1 egg yolk
½ cup chocolate chips, melted
   Slivered almonds, halved

1. Preheat oven to 350°F. Combine hazelnuts, flour, cocoa, cinnamon, nutmeg and salt in medium bowl.

2. Beat 1 cup butter, powdered sugar and egg yolk in large bowl until light and fluffy. Gradually add flour mixture. Beat until soft dough forms.

3. Grease 3 madeleine pans with remaining butter, 1 teaspoon per pan; dust with flour. (If only 1 pan is available, thoroughly wash, dry, regrease and flour after baking each batch. Cover remaining dough with plastic wrap; stand at room temperature.) Press level tablespoonfuls of dough into each mold.

4. Bake 12 minutes or until centers are set. Let stand in pan 3 minutes. Loosen cookies from pan with point of small knife. Invert pan over wire rack; tap lightly to release cookies. Let stand 2 minutes. Cool completely shell-side up.

5. Pipe melted chocolate on curved end of each cookie; place slivered almond halves in melted chocolate for claws. Let stand at room temperature 1 hour or until set.

6. Store tightly covered at room temperature.

Makes about 5 dozen cookies

Note: These cookies do not freeze well.

Czech Bear Paws

Peppermint Pigs

1 package (18 ounces) refrigerated sugar cookie dough
½ cup all-purpose flour
¾ teaspoon peppermint extract
Red food coloring
Prepared white icing and mini candy-coated chocolate pieces

1. Preheat oven to 350°F. Lightly grease cookie sheets.

2. Remove dough from wrapper; place in large bowl. Let dough stand at room temperature about 15 minutes.

3. Add flour, peppermint extract and food coloring to dough; beat at medium speed of electric mixer until well blended and evenly colored. Divide dough into 20 equal pieces.

4. For each pig, shape 1 dough piece into 1 (1-inch) ball, 1 (½-inch) ball and 2 (¼-inch) balls. Flatten 1-inch ball to ¼-inch-thick round; place on prepared cookie sheet. Flatten ½-inch ball to ¼-inch-thick oval; place on top of dough round for snout. Shape 2 (¼-inch) balls into triangles; fold point over and place at top of round for ears. Make indentations in snout with wooden skewer for nostrils.

5. Bake 9 to 11 minutes or until set. Remove to wire racks; cool completely. Use white icing and candy-coated chocolate pieces to make eyes. *Makes 20 cookies*

Peppermint Pigs

Myrtle the Turtle

¾ cup (1½ sticks) unsalted butter, softened
¼ cup *each* granulated sugar and packed light brown sugar
1 egg yolk
1¾ cups all-purpose flour
¾ teaspoon baking powder
⅛ teaspoon salt
Green food coloring
Assorted colored hard candies, crushed*
Prepared colored icings, small candies and decors

*To crush hard candies, unwrap and place each color in separate heavy resealable plastic food storage bag; seal bags. Crush with rolling pin or hammer.

1. Beat butter, sugars and egg yolk in bowl until blended. Stir in flour, baking powder and salt until blended. Tint dough with food coloring; shape into disc. Wrap in plastic wrap; chill 1 hour.

2. Preheat oven to 350°F. Line cookie sheets with foil; lightly grease foil. Roll dough on lightly floured surface to ¼-inch thickness. For turtle shells, cut 6 circles with 4-inch round cookie cutter; cut circles in half. Place shells 2 inches apart on prepared cookie sheets. Using mini cookie cutters or knife, cut out shapes from shells in decorative patterns.

3. For heads, cut 12 circles with 1-inch round cookie cutter. Moisten back of head and place at bottom center of shell; press down. For feet, cut 12 circles with ½- to ¾-inch round cookie cutter; cut circles in half. Place feet on prepared cookie sheet near left and right edges of shells; press together to seal. Decorate with candies as desired, or leave plain to decorate after baking. Generously fill cutout shapes in shells with crushed candies.

4. Bake 8 to 10 minutes or until edges are lightly browned and candy is melted. Remove foil and cookies to wire rack; cool completely. Decorate faces and shells with assorted icings, candies and decors as desired.   *Makes 1 dozen cookies*

Myrtle the Turtle

Peanut Butter Critter Cookies

3 cups all-purpose flour
1 cup (2 sticks) butter, softened
1 cup peanut butter chips, melted
¾ cup granulated sugar
¼ cup packed brown sugar
1 egg
1½ teaspoons milk
1 teaspoon vanilla
Powdered sugar
Prepared colored icings

1. Combine flour, butter, melted peanut butter chips, granulated sugar, brown sugar, egg, milk and vanilla in large bowl. Beat at low speed of electric mixer 1 to 2 minutes, scraping bowl often, until well blended. Divide dough in half. Wrap in plastic wrap; refrigerate 1 to 2 hours or until firm.

2. Preheat oven to 375°F. Roll out dough on well-floured surface to ⅛-inch thickness. Cut desired shapes using 2½-inch cookie cutters. Place 1 inch apart on ungreased cookie sheets. Bake 5 to 8 minutes or until edges are lightly browned. Remove immediately to wire racks; cool completely. Sprinkle with powdered sugar or decorate with icings as desired.

Makes about 4 dozen cookies

Chocolate Bunny Cookies

1 (21-ounce) package DUNCAN HINES® Family-Style Chewy Fudge Brownie Mix
1 egg
¼ cup water
¼ cup vegetable oil
1⅓ cups pecan halves (96)
1 container DUNCAN HINES® Creamy Home-Style Dark Chocolate Fudge Frosting
White chocolate chips

1. Preheat oven to 350°F. Grease baking sheets.

2. Combine brownie mix, egg, water and oil in large bowl. Stir with spoon until well blended, about 50 strokes. Drop by level tablespoonfuls 2 inches apart on greased baking sheets. Place two pecan halves, flat-side up, on each cookie for ears. Bake at 350°F for 10 to 12 minutes or until set. Cool 2 minutes on baking sheets. Remove to cooling racks. Cool completely.

3. Spread Dark Chocolate Fudge frosting on one cookie. Place white chocolate chips, upside down, on frosting for eyes and nose. Dot each eye with frosting using toothpick. Repeat for remaining cookies. Allow frosting to set before storing cookies between layers of waxed paper in airtight container.

Makes 4 dozen cookies

Tip: To make white bunnies, frost cookies with Duncan Hines® Vanilla Frosting and use semisweet chocolate chips for the eyes and noses.

Chocolate Bunny Cookies

Finnish Spice Cookies

- **2 cups all-purpose flour**
- **1½ teaspoons ground ginger**
- **1½ teaspoons ground cinnamon**
- **½ teaspoon ground cardamom**
- **½ teaspoon ground cloves**
- **⅔ cup packed light brown sugar**
- **½ cup (1 stick) butter, softened**
- **½ teaspoon baking soda**
- **3 to 5 tablespoons hot water**
- **Royal Icing (recipe follows)**

1. Combine flour, ginger, cinnamon, cardamom and cloves in medium bowl.

2. Beat brown sugar and butter in large bowl until light and fluffy. Dissolve baking soda in 3 tablespoons water in cup. Beat into butter mixture. Gradually add flour mixture. Beat until dough forms. (If dough is too crumbly, add more water, 1 tablespoon at a time, until dough holds together.) Form dough into 2 discs; wrap in plastic wrap and refrigerate until firm, 30 minutes or overnight.

3. Preheat oven to 375°F. Grease cookie sheets.

4. Working with 1 disc at a time, roll out dough on lightly floured surface to ⅛-inch thickness. Cut dough with floured 3-inch pig-shaped cookie cutter or desired cookie cutter. Place cutouts 1 inch apart on prepared cookie sheets. Gather dough scraps; reroll and cut out more cookies.

5. Bake 8 to 10 minutes or until firm and edges are lightly browned. Remove to wire rack; cool completely.

6. Prepare Royal Icing. Spoon icing into pastry bag fitted with writing tip. Decorate cooled cookies with icing. Let stand at room temperature 1 hour or until set. Store tightly covered at room temperature or freeze up to 3 months.

Makes about 5 dozen cookies

Royal Icing

1 egg white,* at room temperature
2 to 2½ cups sifted powdered sugar
½ teaspoon almond extract

*Use only Grade A clean, uncracked egg.

1. Beat egg white in small bowl at high speed of electric mixture until foamy.

2. Gradually add 2 cups powdered sugar and almond extract. Beat at low speed until moistened. Increase mixer speed to high and beat until icing is stiff. If icing is too thin, add additional powdered sugar, 1 tablespoon at a time, until of good piping consistency.

Beautiful Butterflies

1 package (18 ounces) refrigerated sugar cookie dough
24 wooden craft sticks
6 squares (1 ounce each) white chocolate
Assorted food colorings
1 cup "M&M's"® Chocolate Mini Baking Bits

Preheat oven to 325°F. Working with half the dough at a time on lightly floured surface, roll to ¼-inch thickness. Cut into butterfly shapes using 3-inch cookie cutter. Press onto craft sticks and place about 2 inches apart on ungreased cookie sheets. Bake 10 to 12 minutes. Cool 2 minutes on cookie sheets; cool completely on wire racks. In top of double boiler over hot water melt white chocolate. Remove from heat; divide among separate bowls for each glaze color desired. Tint with food colorings as desired. Spread colored white chocolate over cookies; decorate with "M&M's"® Chocolate Mini Baking Bits. Let set. Store in tightly covered container.

Makes 2 dozen cookies

Gingerbread Bears

3½ cups all-purpose flour
2 teaspoons ground cinnamon
1½ teaspoons ground ginger
1 teaspoon *each* salt, baking soda and ground allspice
1 cup (2 sticks) butter, softened
1 cup packed light brown sugar
1 teaspoon vanilla
⅓ cup molasses
2 eggs
Assorted decors (optional)
Prepared creamy or gel-type frostings in tubes (optional)
Colored sugars and assorted candies (optional)

1. Combine flour, cinnamon, ginger, salt, baking soda and allspice in medium bowl.

2. Beat butter, brown sugar and vanilla in large bowl at medium speed of electric mixer about 5 minutes or until light and fluffy. Beat in molasses and eggs until well blended. Beat in flour mixture at low speed until well blended. Divide dough into 3 equal portions. Wrap in plastic wrap; refrigerate at least 2 hours or up to 24 hours.

3. Preheat oven to 350°F. Grease large cookie sheets. Working with 1 portion at a time, roll out dough on lightly floured surface to ⅛-inch thickness. Cut dough with 3-inch bear-shaped cookie cutter. Place cutouts 1 inch apart on prepared cookie sheets. Roll dough scraps into small balls and ropes to make eyes and noses and to decorate bears. Decorate bears with decors, if desired. Bake 10 minutes or until edges are lightly browned. Cool on cookie sheets 1 minute. Remove to wire rack; cool completely.

4. Pipe or spread frosting on cooled cookies and decorate with assorted decors, colored sugars and candies, if desired.

Makes about 3½ dozen cookies

Gingerbread Bears

Fun to Make & Fun to Eat

Chocolate Peanut Butter Cookies

1 package DUNCAN HINES® Moist Deluxe® Devil's Food
   Cake Mix
¾ cup crunchy peanut butter
2 eggs
2 tablespoons milk
1 cup candy-coated peanut butter pieces

1. Preheat oven to 350°F. Grease baking sheets.

2. Combine cake mix, peanut butter, eggs and milk in large mixing bowl. Beat at low speed with electric mixer until blended. Stir in peanut butter pieces.

3. Drop dough by slightly rounded tablespoonfuls onto prepared baking sheets. Bake 7 to 9 minutes or until lightly browned. Cool 2 minutes on baking sheets. Remove to cooling racks. *Makes about 3½ dozen cookies*

Variation: If desired, use 1 cup peanut butter chips in place of peanut butter pieces.

Mud Puddle Pie

**1 package (18 ounces) refrigerated chocolate chip cookie
    dough
Red, orange and yellow decorator icings
¼ cup chocolate chips, melted
2 tablespoons cocoa powder
1 can (15¾ ounces) chocolate pudding
Gummy worms or gummy insects**

1. Preheat oven to 350°F. Remove dough from wrapper, keeping in log shape. Cut off 1½-inch portion of dough. Place remaining dough in large bowl; set aside.

2. Shape small dough portion into 3 to 4 leaves. Place 2 inches apart on ungreased cookie sheet. Bake 4 to 6 minutes or until edges are lightly browned. Remove to wire rack; cool completely. Decorate with red, orange and yellow icings as desired. Pipe melted chocolate onto leaves for veins. Let stand until set.

3. Generously grease 12-inch pizza pan. Add cocoa to dough; beat at medium speed of electric mixer until well blended. Press dough into prepared pan, leaving about ¾-inch space between dough and edge of pan. Bake 9 to 11 minutes or until center is set. Cool completely in pan on wire rack. Run metal spatula between cookie and pan after 10 to 15 minutes to loosen.

4. Spread pudding over cookie to within 1 inch of edge. Top with gummy worms and leaf cookies. Cut into wedges to serve. *Makes 12 servings*

Mud Puddle Pie

Chocolate Cherry Slices

⅓ cup red maraschino cherries, well drained
⅓ cup green maraschino cherries, well drained
2 packages (18 ounces each) refrigerated sugar cookie dough
⅔ cup all-purpose flour, divided
Red and green food colorings
3 tablespoons cocoa powder

1. Pat red cherries dry with paper towels. Finely chop; place in small bowl. Repeat with green cherries, placing in separate bowl.

2. Remove dough from wrappers, keeping in log shapes. Cut each dough log into thirds, making six pieces total. Let dough stand at room temperature about 15 minutes.

3. Combine 2 dough pieces, ⅓ cup flour and red food coloring in medium bowl; beat until well blended and evenly colored. Stir in red cherries. Repeat with 2 dough pieces, remaining ⅓ cup flour, green food coloring and green cherries. Wrap doughs separately in plastic wrap; refrigerate 15 minutes.

4. Combine remaining 2 dough pieces and cocoa powder in medium bowl; beat until well blended. Wrap in plastic wrap; refrigerate 15 minutes.

5. Line 8×4×2-inch loaf pan with plastic wrap, extending wrap over sides. Pat red dough in even layer in prepared pan. Pat chocolate dough in even layer over red dough. Pat green dough in even layer over chocolate dough. Wrap plastic wrap tightly around dough. Freeze 2 hours.

6. Preheat oven to 350°F. Remove dough from pan; cut in half lengthwise. Cut each half into ¼-inch-thick slices. Place slices 2 inches apart on ungreased cookie sheets. Bake 10 to 12 minutes or until set. Cool on cookie sheets 1 minute. Remove to wire rack; cool completely.

Makes about 5 dozen cookies

Chocolate Cherry Slices

Maple Oatmeal Raisin Drops

1 package (18 ounces) refrigerated sugar cookie dough
1 cup uncooked quick oats
1 cup raisins
¼ cup maple syrup
   Maple Glaze (recipe follows)

1. Preheat oven to 350°F. Lightly grease cookie sheets.

2. Remove dough from wrapper; place in large bowl. Let dough stand at room temperature about 15 minutes.

3. Add oats, raisins and maple syrup to dough; beat at medium speed of electric mixer until well blended. Drop by rounded teaspoonfuls 2 inches apart onto prepared cookie sheets.

4. Bake 9 to 11 minutes or until edges are lightly browned and center is set. Cool on cookie sheets 1 minute. Remove to wire rack; cool completely.

5. Prepare Maple Glaze; drizzle over cooled cookies. Let stand until set.   *Makes 3 dozen cookies*

Maple Glaze: Combine 1 cup powdered sugar and 1 tablespoon maple syrup in small bowl; whisk until blended. If necessary, add additional maple syrup by teaspoonfuls until glaze is of drizzling consistency.

Maple Oatmeal Raisin Drops

Glazed Donut Cookies

1 package (18 ounces) refrigerated oatmeal raisin cookie dough in squares or rounds (12 count)
Prepared white or chocolate frosting
Assorted colored sprinkles

1. Preheat oven to 350°F. Grease 12 (2½- or 2¾-inch) muffin pan cups.

2. Remove dough from wrapper; separate into 12 pieces. Let dough stand at room temperature about 15 minutes.

3. Shape each dough piece into 12-inch-long rope on lightly floured surface. Coil ropes into muffin cups, leaving centers open.

4. Bake 12 minutes; remove from oven and re-shape center hole with round handle of wooden spoon. Return to oven; bake 3 to 4 minutes or until set.

5. Remove from oven; re-shape holes, if necessary. Cool in pan 4 minutes. Remove to wire rack; cool completely.

6. Spread frosting over cookies; decorate with sprinkles.

Makes 12 large cookies

S'More Bars

1 package (18 ounces) refrigerated chocolate chip cookie dough
¼ cup graham cracker crumbs
3 cups mini marshmallows
½ cup semisweet or milk chocolate chips
2 teaspoons shortening

1. Preheat oven to 350°F. Grease 13×9×2-inch baking pan.

2. Remove dough from wrapper. Press dough into prepared pan. Sprinkle with graham cracker crumbs.

3. Bake 10 to 12 minutes or until edges are golden brown. Sprinkle with marshmallows. Bake 2 to 3 minutes or until marshmallows are puffed. Cool completely in pan on wire rack.

4. Combine chocolate chips and shortening in small resealable plastic food storage bag; seal bag. Microwave at HIGH (100% power) 1 minute; knead bag lightly. Microwave at HIGH for additional 30-second intervals until chips and shortening are completely melted and smooth, kneading bag after each interval. Cut off tiny corner of bag. Drizzle over bars. Refrigerate 5 to 10 minutes or until chocolate is set.

Makes 3 dozen bars

Try cutting these scrumptious bar cookies into triangles or diamonds for a festive new shape. To make serving them easier, remove a corner piece first and then remove the rest.

S'More Bars

Cinnamon Swirls

1 package (18 ounces) refrigerated sugar cookie dough
½ cup packed light brown sugar
2 teaspoons ground cinnamon
1 cup powdered sugar
2 to 3 tablespoons milk
½ cup finely chopped walnuts or pecans (optional)

1. Remove dough from wrapper; divide dough in half. Wrap 1 dough half in plastic wrap; refrigerate. Place remaining dough half in medium bowl. Let dough stand at room temperature about 15 minutes.

2. Add brown sugar and cinnamon to dough in bowl; beat at medium speed of electric mixer until well blended. Wrap dough in plastic wrap; refrigerate until needed.

3. Roll plain dough on lightly floured surface to form 8-inch square. Repeat with cinnamon dough; place cinnamon dough on top of plain dough. Roll up doughs into 10-inch log. Wrap log in plastic wrap; freeze 1 hour.

4. Preheat oven to 350°F. Grease cookie sheets. Cut dough log into ⅜-inch slices; place on prepared cookie sheets. Bake 10 to 12 minutes or until edges are lightly browned. Remove to wire rack; cool completely.

5. For icing, mix powdered sugar and 2 tablespoons milk in small bowl until smooth. If necessary, add additional milk, 1 teaspoon at a time, until of desired drizzling consistency. Drizzle icing over cooled cookies; sprinkle with nuts, if desired.

Makes 2 dozen cookies

Cinnamon Swirls

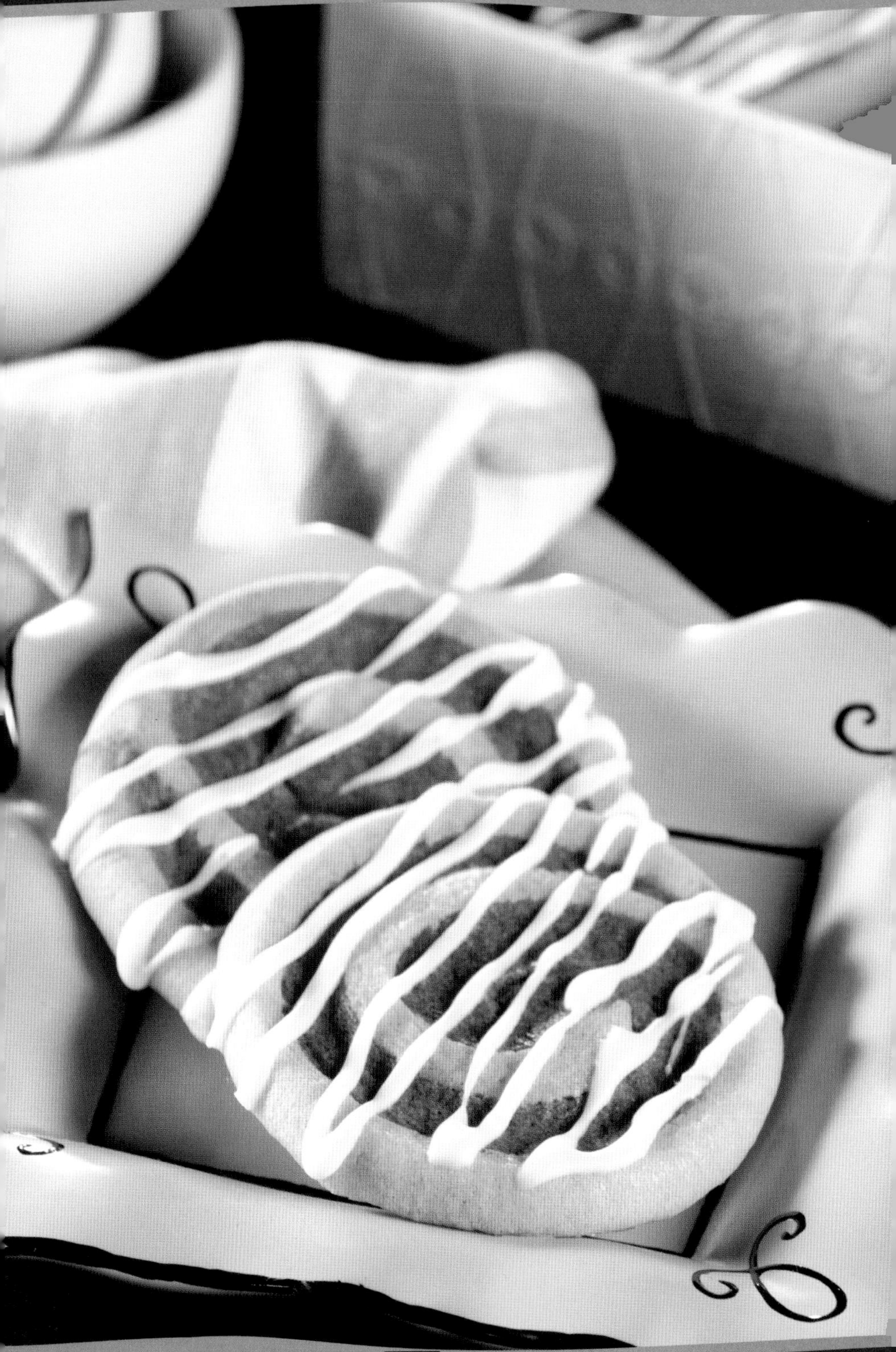

Jammy Streusel Bars

1 package (18 ounces) refrigerated sugar cookie dough
½ cup strawberry, raspberry or blackberry jam
½ cup all-purpose flour
½ cup packed light brown sugar
¼ cup (½ stick) butter or margarine
1 cup sliced almonds or chopped walnuts

1. Preheat oven to 350°F. Grease 13×9-inch baking pan.

2. Remove dough from wrapper; place in prepared pan. Let dough stand at room temperature about 15 minutes.

3. Press dough evenly into pan. Spread jam over dough; set aside.

4. Combine flour and brown sugar in medium bowl; cut in butter with pastry blender or two knives until mixture is crumbly. Sprinkle flour mixture over jam layer. Sprinkle with nuts.

5. Bake 25 minutes or until top and edges are lightly browned. Cool completely in pan on wire rack.

Makes 2½ dozen bars

Peanut Butter S'Mores

1½ cups all-purpose flour
½ teaspoon baking powder
½ teaspoon baking soda
¼ teaspoon salt
½ cup (1 stick) butter, softened
½ cup *each* granulated sugar and packed light brown sugar
½ cup creamy or chunky peanut butter
1 egg
1 teaspoon vanilla
½ cup chopped roasted peanuts (optional)
4 milk chocolate candy bars (1.55 ounces each)
16 large marshmallows

1. Preheat oven to 350°F.

2. Combine flour, baking powder, baking soda and salt in small bowl; set aside. Beat butter, granulated sugar and brown sugar in large bowl at medium speed of electric mixer until light and fluffy. Add peanut butter, egg and vanilla; beat until well blended. Gradually beat in flour mixture at low speed until blended. Stir in peanuts, if desired.

3. Shape dough into 1-inch balls; place 2 inches apart on ungreased cookie sheets. Flatten dough with fork, creating criss-cross pattern. Bake about 14 minutes or until set and edges are lightly browned. Cool cookies 2 minutes on cookie sheets. Remove to wire rack; cool completely.

4. To assemble sandwiches, break each candy bar into four sections. Place 1 section of chocolate on flat side of 1 cookie. Place on microwavable plate; top with 1 marshmallow. Microwave at HIGH 10 to 12 seconds or until marshmallow is puffy. Immediately top with another cookie, flat side down. Press lightly on top cookie, spreading marshmallow to edges. Repeat with remaining cookies, marshmallows and candy pieces, one at a time.   *Makes 16 sandwich cookies*

Peanut Butter S'Mores

Fruit & Nut Molasses Crescents

1 package (18 ounces) refrigerated sugar cookie dough
6 tablespoons all-purpose flour
2 tablespoons packed light brown sugar
2 tablespoons dark molasses
½ teaspoon ground cinnamon
½ teaspoon ground ginger
1¼ cups trail mix with nuts, raisins and candy-coated
   chocolate pieces, coarsely chopped
Melted white or dark chocolate (optional)

1. Remove dough from wrapper; place in large bowl. Let dough stand at room temperature about 15 minutes.

2. Add flour, brown sugar, molasses, cinnamon and ginger to dough; beat at medium speed of electric mixer until well blended. Divide dough into 4 equal pieces. Wrap pieces individually in plastic wrap; refrigerate at least 2 hours.

3. Preheat oven to 325°F. Grease cookie sheets. Roll 1 dough piece into 7-inch circle on lightly floured surface. Sprinkle with 5 tablespoons trail mix. Cut dough into 5 wedges. Roll each wedge from wide end in towards point. Gently shape into crescent. Place crescents 2 inches apart on prepared cookie sheets. Fill sides of crescents with any trail mix that spills out. Repeat with remaining dough and trail mix to make 20 crescents.

4. Bake 12 to 15 minutes or until edges are lightly browned. Cool on cookie sheets 5 minutes. Place waxed paper under wire rack. Remove crescents to wire rack. Drizzle with melted chocolate, if desired. Let stand until set.

Makes 20 crescents

Fruit & Nut Molasses Crescents

Coconut Snowdrops

1 package (18 ounces) refrigerated chocolate chip cookie
    dough or peanut butter chocolate chip cookie dough
¼ cup unsweetened cocoa powder
2 tablespoons packed light brown sugar
2 cups toasted coconut*
¾ cup marshmallow creme

*To toast coconut, spread evenly on ungreased cookie sheet. Toast in preheated 350°F oven 5 to 7 minutes, stirring occasionally until light golden brown.

1. Preheat oven to 350°F. Grease cookie sheets. Remove dough from wrapper; place in large bowl. Let dough stand at room temperature about 15 minutes.

2. Add cocoa and brown sugar to dough in bowl; beat at medium speed of electric mixer until well blended.

3. Shape dough into 40 balls; place 1-inch apart on prepared cookie sheets. Bake 11 to 13 minutes or until puffed and slightly firm. Cool on cookie sheets 3 minutes. Remove to wire rack; cool completely.

4. Place toasted coconut on plate. Spread 1 rounded teaspoon marshmallow creme on top of each cookie; dip into coconut to coat. *Makes 40 cookies*

Variation: Substitute 1 cup creamy peanut butter for marshmallow creme.

Coconut Snowdrops

Crispy's Irresistible Peanut Butter Marbles

**1 package (18 ounces) refrigerated peanut butter cookie
   dough**
2 cups "M&M's"® Milk Chocolate Mini Baking Bits, divided
1 cup crisp rice cereal, divided (optional)
1 package (18 ounces) refrigerated sugar cookie dough
¼ cup unsweetened cocoa powder

In large bowl combine peanut butter dough, 1 cup "M&M's"®
Milk Chocolate Mini Baking Bits and ½ cup cereal, if desired.
Remove dough to small bowl; set aside. In large bowl combine
sugar dough and cocoa powder until well blended. Stir in
remaining 1 cup "M&M's"® Milk Chocolate Mini Baking Bits
and remaining ½ cup cereal, if desired. Remove half the
dough to small bowl; set aside. Combine half the peanut
butter dough with half the chocolate dough by folding
together just enough to marble. Shape marbled dough into
8×2-inch log. Wrap log in plastic wrap. Repeat with remaining
doughs. Refrigerate logs 2 hours. To bake, preheat oven to
350°F. Cut dough into ¼-inch-thick slices. Place about 2 inches
apart on ungreased cookie sheets. Bake 12 to 14 minutes. Cool
1 minute on cookie sheets; cool completely on wire racks.
Store in tightly covered container.   *Makes 5 dozen cookies*

Crispy's Irresistible
Peanut Butter Marbles

Sweet Nutty O's

1 cup finely chopped honey-roasted peanuts, divided
1 package (18 ounces) refrigerated sugar cookie dough
¼ cup all-purpose flour
2 tablespoons honey
1 egg white, lightly beaten

1. Preheat oven to 350°F. Lightly grease cookie sheets. Reserve ¼ cup peanuts. Remove dough from wrapper; place in large bowl. Let dough stand at room temperature about 15 minutes.

2. Add remaining ¾ cup peanuts, flour and honey to dough; beat at medium speed of electric mixer until well blended.

3. For each cookie, shape about 1 tablespoon dough into 4-inch-long rope. Press ends together to make ring; place on prepared cookie sheets. Brush with egg white; press reserved peanuts into rings.

4. Bake 9 to 11 minutes or until edges are lightly browned. Cool on cookie sheets 1 minute. Remove to wire rack; cool completely.   *Makes 3 dozen cookies*

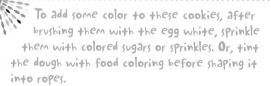

To add some color to these cookies, after brushing them with the egg white, sprinkle them with colored sugars or sprinkles. Or, tint the dough with food coloring before shaping it into ropes.

Sweet Nutty O's

Chocolate Malt Delights

**1 package (18 ounces) refrigerated chocolate chip cookie
    dough**
**⅓ cup plus 3 tablespoons malted milk powder, original or
    chocolate flavor, divided**
1¼ cups prepared chocolate frosting
1 cup coarsely chopped malted milk balls

1. Preheat oven to 350°F. Grease cookie sheets.

2. Remove dough from wrapper; place in large bowl. Let
dough stand at room temperature about 15 minutes.

3. Add ⅓ cup malted milk powder to dough; beat at medium
speed of electric mixer until well blended. Drop rounded
tablespoons of dough 2 inches apart onto prepared
cookie sheets.

4. Bake 10 to 12 minutes or until edges are lightly browned.
Cool on cookie sheets 5 minutes. Remove to wire rack; cool
completely.

5. Combine frosting and remaining 3 tablespoons malted milk
powder. Top each cookie with rounded tablespoon of frosting;
garnish with malted milk balls.   *Makes 1½ dozen cookies*

Chocolate Malt Delights

Ultimate Rocky Road Cups

¾ cup (1½ sticks) butter or margarine
4 squares (1 ounce each) unsweetened baking chocolate
1½ cups granulated sugar
3 eggs
1 cup all-purpose flour
1¾ cups "M&M's"® Chocolate Mini Baking Bits
¾ cup coarsely chopped peanuts
1 cup mini marshmallows

Preheat oven to 350°F. Generously grease 24 (2½-inch) muffin cups or line with foil liners. Place butter and chocolate in large microwave-safe bowl. Microwave on HIGH 1 minute; stir. Microwave on HIGH an additional 30 seconds; stir until chocolate is completely melted. Add sugar and eggs, one at a time, beating well after each addition; blend in flour. In separate bowl combine "M&M's"® Chocolate Mini Baking Bits and nuts; stir 1 cup baking bits mixture into brownie batter. Divide batter evenly among prepared muffin cups. Bake 20 minutes. Combine remaining baking bits mixture with marshmallows; divide evenly among muffin cups, topping hot brownies. Return to oven; bake 5 minutes longer. Cool completely before removing from muffin cups. Store in tightly covered container.   *Makes 24 cups*

Ultimate Rocky Road Squares: Prepare recipe as directed, spreading batter into generously greased 13×9×2-inch baking pan. Bake 30 minutes. Sprinkle with topping mixture; bake 5 minutes longer. Cool completely. Cut into squares. Store in tightly covered container. Makes 24 squares.

Ultimate Rocky Road Cups

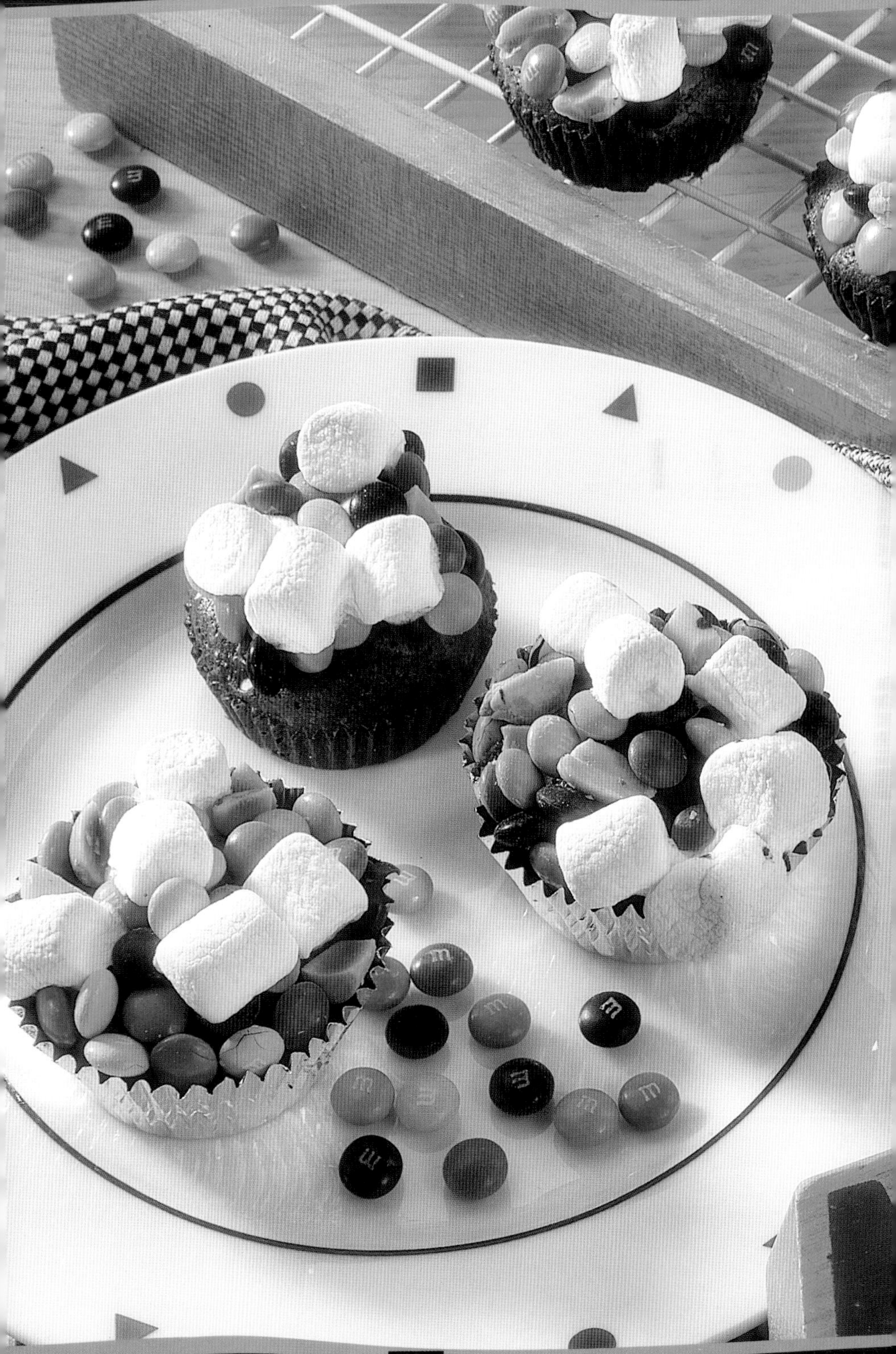

Chocolate Peanut Fudge Bars

1 package (18 ounces) refrigerated chocolate chip cookie
    dough with peanut butter filling in squares or rounds
    (20 count)
1 package (12 ounces) semisweet chocolate chips
1 cup heavy cream
3 egg yolks, beaten
½ cup all-purpose flour
¼ cup uncooked old-fashioned oats
¼ cup packed light brown sugar
3 tablespoons butter
½ cup coarsely chopped salted peanuts

1. Preheat oven to 350°F. Grease 13×9-inch baking pan. Remove dough from wrapper; place in prepared pan. Let dough stand at room temperature about 15 minutes.

2. Press dough evenly into pan. Bake 10 minutes. Remove from oven.

3. Combine chocolate chips and cream in small saucepan over low heat. Cook and stir 3 to 4 minutes or until chocolate is melted and mixture is smooth. Remove from heat; stir in egg yolks. Spread chocolate mixture over dough.

4. Combine flour, oats and brown sugar in medium bowl. Cut in butter with pastry blender or two knives until mixture is crumbly. Stir in chopped peanuts. Sprinkle over chocolate layer. Return to oven 25 to 30 minutes or until just firm. Cool completely in pan on wire rack. *Makes 2 dozen bars*

Chocolate Peanut Fudge Bars

Cookie Pizza

1 (18-ounce) package refrigerated sugar cookie dough
2 cups (12 ounces) semi-sweet chocolate chips
1 (14-ounce) can EAGLE BRAND® Sweetened Condensed
 Milk (NOT evaporated milk)
2 cups candy-coated milk chocolate pieces
2 cups miniature marshmallows
½ cup peanuts

1. Preheat oven to 375°F. Press cookie dough into 2 ungreased 12-inch pizza pans. Bake 10 minutes or until golden. Remove from oven.

2. In medium saucepan, melt chips with Eagle Brand. Spread over crusts. Sprinkle with chocolate pieces, marshmallows and peanuts.

3. Bake 4 minutes or until marshmallows are lightly toasted. Cool. Cut into wedges.   *Makes 2 pizzas (24 servings)*

Prep Time: 15 minutes
Bake Time: 14 minutes

PB & J Cookie Sandwiches

½ cup (1 stick) butter or margarine, softened
½ cup creamy peanut butter
¼ cup solid vegetable shortening
1 cup firmly packed light brown sugar
1 egg
1 teaspoon vanilla extract
1⅔ cups all-purpose flour
1 teaspoon baking soda
½ teaspoon baking powder
1 cup "M&M's"® Milk Chocolate Mini Baking Bits
½ cup finely chopped peanuts
½ cup grape or strawberry jam

Preheat oven to 350°F. In large bowl cream butter, peanut butter, shortening and sugar until light and fluffy; beat in egg and vanilla. In medium bowl combine flour, baking soda and baking powder; blend into creamed mixture. Stir in "M&M's"® Milk Chocolate Mini Baking Bits and nuts. Drop by rounded teaspoonfuls onto ungreased cookie sheets. Bake 8 to 10 minutes or until light golden brown. Let cool 2 minutes on cookie sheets; remove to wire racks to cool completely. Just before serving, spread ½ teaspoon jam on bottom of one cookie; top with second cookie. Store in tightly covered container.   *Makes about 2 dozen sandwich cookies*

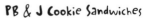

PB & J Cookie Sandwiches

Celebrating the Holidays

Springtime Nests

   1 cup butterscotch chips
   ½ cup light corn syrup
   ½ cup creamy peanut butter
   ⅓ cup sugar
 2½ cups chow mein noodles
   2 cups cornflakes, lightly crushed
      Jelly beans or malted milk egg candies

1. Combine butterscotch chips, corn syrup, peanut butter and sugar in large microwavable bowl. Microwave at HIGH (100% power) 1 to 1½ minutes or until melted and smooth, stirring at 30-second intervals.

2. Stir in chow mein noodles and cornflakes until evenly coated. Quickly shape scant ¼ cupfuls mixture into balls; make indentation in centers to make nests. Place nests on waxed paper to set. Place 3 jelly beans in each nest.

Makes 1½ dozen treats

Eggs-Cellent Easter Cookies

1 package (18 ounces) refrigerated sugar cookie dough
1 cup plus 1 tablespoon powdered sugar, divided
¼ cup all-purpose flour
1 teaspoon almond extract
   Blue food coloring
   Blue sugar (optional)
1 package (3 ounces) cream cheese, softened
1 tablespoon butter, softened
   Red food coloring
½ cup shredded sweetened coconut
   Prepared colored icings and decorating gels (optional)

1. Preheat oven to 350°F. Grease 2 cookie sheets. Remove dough from wrapper; place in large bowl. Let dough stand at room temperature about 15 minutes.

2. Add 1 tablespoon powdered sugar, flour, almond extract and blue food coloring to dough; beat at medium speed of electric mixer until well blended and evenly colored.

3. Shape dough into 40 (2½-inch-long) egg shapes; roll in blue sugar, if desired. Place 2 inches apart on prepared cookie sheets.

4. Bake 8 to 10 minutes or until set and edges are lightly browned. Cool on cookie sheets 2 minutes. Remove to wire rack; cool completely.

5. Combine cream cheese, butter and remaining 1 cup powdered sugar in medium bowl; beat at medium speed of electric mixer until smooth. Tint filling pink with red food coloring. Stir in coconut.

6. Spread pink filling on 20 cookies. Top with remaining 20 cookies to make sandwiches. Decorate tops of sandwiches as desired with colored icings and gels. Let stand until set. Store in refrigerator.   *Makes 20 sandwich cookies*

Eggs-Cellent Easter Cookies

Citrus Easter Chicks

1 package (18 ounces) refrigerated sugar cookie dough
⅓ cup all-purpose flour
1½ to 2 teaspoons lemon extract
Lemon Cookie Glaze (recipe follows)
2 cups shredded coconut, tinted yellow*
Mini chocolate chips and assorted decors

*To tint coconut, combine small amount of food coloring (paste or liquid) with 1 teaspoon water in large bowl. Add coconut and stir until evenly coated. Add more food coloring, if needed.

1. Remove dough from wrapper; place in large bowl. Let dough stand at room temperature about 15 minutes.

2. Add flour and lemon extract to dough; beat until well blended. Divide dough in half. Wrap each half in plastic wrap; freeze 30 minutes.

3. Preheat oven to 350°F. Roll 1 dough half on lightly floured surface to ¼-inch thickness. Cut dough with 2- to 3-inch chick cookie cutters. Place cutouts 2 inches apart on ungreased cookie sheets. Repeat with remaining dough.

4. Bake 7 to 9 minutes or until firm but not browned. Cool on cookie sheets 5 minutes. Remove to wire rack; cool completely.

5. Place wire rack over waxed paper. Prepare Lemon Cookie Glaze. Spread glaze on tops of cookies; sprinkle with yellow coconut. Decorate chicks with chocolate chips and decors as desired. Let stand about 40 minutes or until completely set.

Makes about 1½ dozen cookies

Lemon Cookie Glaze: Combine 4 cups powdered sugar, ¾ teaspoon lemon extract and enough milk (4 to 6 tablespoons), 1 tablespoon at a time to make medium-thick pourable glaze. Tint glaze yellow with food coloring, a few drops at a time, until desired color is achieved.

Citrus Easter Chicks

Uncle Sam's Hat

**1 package (18 ounces) refrigerated chocolate chip cookie
dough**
2 cups powdered sugar
2 to 4 tablespoons milk
Red and blue food colorings

1. Preheat oven to 350°F. Lightly grease 12-inch round pizza pan and cookie sheet. Remove dough from wrapper. Press dough evenly into prepared pizza pan. Cut dough into hat shape as shown in photo. Press scraps together and flatten heaping tablespoons dough onto prepared cookie sheet. Using 1½- to 2-inch star cookie cutter, cut out 3 stars; remove and discard dough scraps.

2. Bake stars 5 to 7 minutes and hat 7 to 9 minutes or until edges are lightly browned. Cool stars on cookie sheet 1 minute. Remove stars to wire rack; cool completely. Cool hat completely on pan on wire rack.

3. Combine powdered sugar and enough milk, 1 tablespoon at a time, to make medium-thick pourable glaze. Spread small amount of glaze over stars and place on waxed paper; let stand until glaze is set. Using red and blue food colorings, tint ½ of glaze red, tint ¼ of glaze blue and leave remaining ¼ of glaze white.

4. Decorate hat with red, white and blue glazes as shown in photo; place stars on blue band of hat. Let stand until glaze is set. *Makes 1 large cookie*

Uncle Sam's Hat

Flag Cookies

1 package (18 ounces) refrigerated sugar cookie dough
Red food coloring
1 aerosol can (6.4 ounces) blue decorating icing, with star
   tip attached
White sprinkles

1. Remove dough from wrapper; divide in half. Wrap 1 half in plastic wrap; refrigerate. Place remaining half in medium bowl. Let stand at room temperature about 15 minutes.

2. Add red food coloring to dough in bowl; beat at medium speed of electric mixer until evenly colored. Wrap in plastic wrap; refrigerate 20 minutes.

3. Roll red dough on lightly floured surface to form 9-inch square. Repeat with plain dough; place plain dough on top of red dough. Cut square into three (3-inch) strips. Stack strips, alternating colors, to create one rectangular log about 9 inches long and 3 inches wide. Place on flat plate and wrap in plastic wrap; freeze 15 minutes or until firm.

4. Preheat oven to 350°F. Grease cookie sheets. Cut dough into ⅓-inch slices; place on prepared cookie sheets.

5. Bake 8 to 10 minutes or until edges are lightly browned. Cool on cookie sheets 3 minutes. Remove to wire rack; cool completely.

6. Pipe 1-inch square of blue icing onto upper left corners of cookies; top with sprinkles.

Makes about 1½ dozen cookies

Flag Cookies

Skull & Cross Bones

1 package (21.5 ounces) brownie mix plus ingredients to
    prepare mix
1 egg white
⅛ teaspoon almond extract (optional)
¼ cup sugar
    Red and black decorating gels
1 container (16 ounces) chocolate frosting

1. Prepare and bake brownies in 13×9-inch baking pan according to package directions. Cool completely.

2. Preheat oven to 250°F. Line cookie sheet with parchment paper.

3. Beat egg white in large bowl until foamy. Add almond extract, if desired; beat until soft peaks form. Gradually add sugar; beat until stiff peaks form.

4. Fill pastry bag fitted with medium writing tip with egg white mixture. Pipe 24 skull and cross bones shapes onto prepared cookie sheet. Bake about 12 minutes or until very lightly browned and set. Cool on cookie sheet on wire rack. Carefully remove meringues from parchment paper. Decorate with red gel for eyes and black gel for mouths.

5. Frost brownies and cut into 24 rectangles. Place one meringue on each brownie. *Makes 2 dozen brownies*

Pumpkin Chocolate Chip Sandwiches

1 cup solid-pack pumpkin
1 package (18 ounces) refrigerated chocolate chip cookie dough
¾ cup all-purpose flour
½ teaspoon pumpkin pie spice*
½ cup prepared cream cheese frosting

*Substitute ¼ teaspoon ground cinnamon, ⅛ teaspoon ground ginger and pinch each ground allspice and ground nutmeg for ½ teaspoon pumpkin pie spice.

1. Line colander with paper towel. Place pumpkin in prepared colander; drain about 20 minutes to remove excess moisture.

2. Preheat oven to 350°F. Grease cookie sheets. Remove dough from wrapper; place in large bowl. Let dough stand at room temperature about 15 minutes.

3. Add pumpkin, flour and pumpkin pie spice to dough; beat at medium speed of electric mixer until well blended.

4. Drop dough by teaspoonfuls onto prepared cookie sheets. Bake 9 to 11 minutes. Cool on cookie sheets 3 minutes. Remove to wire rack; cool completely.

5. Place about 1 teaspoon frosting on flat side of cookie; top with second cookie. Repeat with remaining cookies and frosting.   *Makes about 2 dozen sandwich cookies*

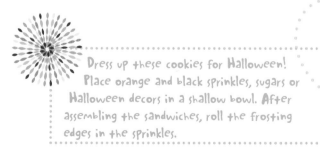

Dress up these cookies for Halloween! Place orange and black sprinkles, sugars or Halloween decors in a shallow bowl. After assembling the sandwiches, roll the frosting edges in the sprinkles.

Pumpkin Chocolate Chip Sandwiches

Smucker's® Spider Web Tartlets

1 (18-ounce) log refrigerated sugar cookie dough
¾ cup all-purpose flour
  CRISCO® Nonstick Cooking Spray or parchment paper
1 cup (12-ounce jar) SMUCKER'S® Apricot Preserves
1 tube black decorating gel

1. Preheat oven to 375°F. Unwrap cookie dough and place in medium mixing bowl. With floured hands, knead flour into cookie dough. Roll dough back into log shape; place on clean cutting board and cut into eight equal slices. With floured fingers, place dough circles on baking sheet lined with parchment paper or sprayed with nonstick spray.

2. Gently press dough circles, flattening to make each one approximately 4 inches in diameter. With thumb and forefinger, pinch edge of each dough circle to create ridge all around. Pinch each dough circle along ridge to make eight points.

3. Spread 2 tablespoons SMUCKER'S® Preserves (or Simply Fruit) onto each dough circle, making sure to spread it all the way to edges and in each point. Refrigerate 20 minutes. Bake 12 to 14 minutes or until edges are lightly browned.

4. Remove tartlets from baking sheet and cool on wire rack. When cool, use black decorating gel to make spider web design. *Makes 8 servings*

Gobbler Cookies

1 package (18 ounces) refrigerated sugar cookie dough
¼ cup all-purpose flour
2 teaspoons ground cinnamon
   White, red, yellow and orange decorating icings
   Chocolate sprinkles, mini chocolate chips and red licorice

1. Preheat oven to 350°F. Lightly grease cookie sheets. Remove dough from wrapper; place in large bowl. Let dough stand at room temperature about 15 minutes.

2. Add flour and cinnamon to dough; beat at medium speed of electric mixer until well blended.

3. Shape dough into 12 (1½-inch) balls, 12 (1-inch balls) and 12 (¾-inch) balls.

4. Flatten large balls into 4-inch rounds on prepared cookie sheets; freeze 10 minutes. Bake 9 to 11 minutes or until edges are lightly browned. Remove to wire rack; cool completely.

5. Flatten medium balls into 2¼-inch rounds on prepared cookie sheets; freeze 10 minutes. Bake 8 to 10 minutes or until edges are lightly browned. Remove to wire rack; cool completely.

6. Flatten small balls into 1-inch rounds on prepared cookie sheets; freeze 10 minutes. Bake 6 to 8 minutes or until edges are lightly browned. Remove to wire rack; cool completely.

7. Decorate large cookies with red, yellow and orange icings and chocolate sprinkles to make feathers. Place medium cookies on large cookies, towards bottom; place small cookies above medium cookies on large cookies. Decorate turkeys as shown in photo using icings, chocolate chips and licorice to make eyes, beaks, gobblers and feet. Let stand 20 minutes or until set. *Makes 1 dozen large cookies*

Hanukkah Coin Cookies

1 cup (2 sticks) butter or margarine, softened
1 cup sugar
1 egg
1 teaspoon vanilla extract
1¾ cups all-purpose flour
½ cup HERSHEY®S Cocoa
1½ teaspoons baking powder
½ teaspoon salt
Buttercream Frosting (recipe follows)

1. Beat butter, sugar, egg and vanilla in bowl until well blended. Stir together flour, cocoa, baking powder and salt; gradually add to butter mixture, beating until well blended. Divide dough in half; place each half on separate sheet of wax paper.

2. Shape each portion into log, about 7 inches long. Wrap each log in wax paper. Refrigerate until firm, at least 8 hours.

3. Heat oven to 325°F. Cut logs into ¼-inch-thick slices. Place on ungreased cookie sheet.

4. Bake 8 to 10 minutes or until set. Cool slightly; remove to wire rack. Cool completely. Prepare Buttercream Frosting; spread over tops of cookies.   *Makes about 4½ dozen cookies*

Buttercream Frosting

¼ cup (½ stick) butter, softened
1½ cups powdered sugar
1 to 2 tablespoons milk
½ teaspoon vanilla extract
Yellow food color

Beat butter until creamy. Gradually add powdered sugar and milk to butter, beating to desired consistency. Stir in vanilla and food color.   *Makes about 1 cup frosting*

Hanukkah Coin Cookies

Hanukkah Cookies

½ cup (1 stick) unsalted butter, softened
1 package (3 ounces) cream cheese, softened
½ cup sugar
¼ cup honey
1 egg
½ teaspoon vanilla
2½ cups all-purpose flour
⅓ cup finely ground walnuts
1 teaspoon baking powder
¼ teaspoon salt
Prepared blue, white and yellow icings

1. Beat butter, cream cheese, sugar, honey, egg and vanilla in large bowl at medium speed of electric mixer until creamy. Stir in flour, walnuts, baking powder and salt until well blended. Form dough into disc; wrap in plastic wrap. Refrigerate about 2 hours or until firm.

2. Preheat oven to 350°F. Lightly grease cookie sheets. Roll out dough, small portion at a time, to ¼-inch thickness on floured surface with lightly floured rolling pin. (Keep remaining dough wrapped in refrigerator until needed.) Cut dough with 2½-inch dreidel-shaped cookie cutter and 6-pointed star cookie cutter. Place 2 inches apart on prepared cookie sheets.

3. Bake 8 to 10 minutes or until edges are lightly browned. Let cookies stand on cookie sheets 1 to 2 minutes. Remove to wire rack; cool completely. Decorate cookies with icings as desired.   *Makes 3½ dozen cookies*

Hanukkah Cookies

Christmas Wreaths

1 package (18 ounces) refrigerated sugar cookie dough
2 tablespoons all-purpose flour
    Green food coloring
    Green colored sugar or sprinkles
    Red decorating icing

1. Remove dough from wrapper; place in large bowl. Let dough stand at room temperature about 15 minutes.

2. Add flour and green food coloring to dough; beat at medium speed of electric mixer until dough well blended and evenly colored. Divide dough in half. Wrap each half in plastic wrap; freeze 20 minutes.

3. Preheat oven to 350°F. Grease cookie sheets. For cookie bottoms, roll 1 dough half on lightly floured surface to ⅜-inch thickness. Cut with 3-inch round or fluted cookie cutter; place 2 inches apart on prepared cookie sheets. Using 1-inch round cookie cutter, cut center circle from each cookie.

4. For cookie tops, roll remaining dough half on lightly floured surface to ⅜-inch thickness. Cut with 3-inch round or fluted cookie cutter; place 2 inches apart on prepared cookie sheets. Using 1-inch round cookie cutter, cut center circle from each cookie. Cut tiny shapes from rings using knife or drinking straw. Sprinkle with green sugar.

5. Bake cutouts 10 minutes or until edges are very lightly browned. Cool on cookie sheets 5 minutes. Remove to wire rack; cool completely.

6. To assemble, spread icing onto flat sides of bottom cookies; place top cookies over icing.

Makes about 1½ dozen sandwich cookies

Fireside Cookie

1 package (18 ounces) refrigerated cookie dough, any flavor
Prepared icings, red licorice bites, black string licorice, gumdrops, mini chocolate chips and assorted candies

1. Preheat oven to 350°F. Line 2 large cookie sheets with parchment paper.

2. Remove dough from wrapper. Using about ¼ of dough, roll into 12×3-inch strip on lightly floured surface. Trim to 11×2¼ inches; set aside. Roll remaining dough into 10×8-inch rectangle. Trim to 9×7¾ inches; place on one prepared cookie sheet. Place reserved dough strip at top of rectangle to make fireplace mantel. Roll remaining scraps; cut into stocking shapes. Place on remaining prepared cookie sheet.

3. Bake 10 minutes or until edges are lightly browned. Cool on cookie sheets 5 minutes. Remove stocking cookies to wire rack. Slide large cookie and parchment paper onto wire rack; cool completely.

4. Decorate with icings and candies as shown, attaching stockings to fireplace cookie with icing.

Makes 1 large cookie

Host a holiday cookie exchange this year! Ask each guest to bring a batch of his or her favorite cookies, enough for everyone to take some home. Bake and decorate this Fireside Cookie as an edible centerpiece.

Fireside Cookie

Yule Tree Namesakes

Butter Cookie Dough (page 208)
Cookie Glaze (page 208)
Green food coloring
1 to 2 tablespoons powdered sugar
Assorted candies
3 packages (12 ounces each) semisweet chocolate chips, melted
1 cup flaked coconut, tinted green*

*To tint coconut, combine small amount of food coloring (paste or liquid) with 1 teaspoon water in large bowl. Add coconut and stir until evenly coated. Add more coloring, if needed.

1. Preheat oven to 350°F. Roll dough on floured surface to ⅛-inch thickness. Cut dough using 3- to 4-inch tree-shaped cookie cutter. Place 2 inches apart on ungreased cookie sheets.

2. Bake 12 to 14 minutes or until edges are lightly browned. Remove to wire rack; cool completely.

3. Reserve ⅓ cup Cookie Glaze; tint remaining glaze with green food coloring. Place cookies on wire rack set over waxed paper-lined cookie sheet. Spoon green glaze over cookies.

4. Add powdered sugar to reserved Cookie Glaze until of piping consistency. Spoon into pastry bag fitted with small writing tip. Pipe names onto trees. Decorate with candies as desired. Let stand until glaze is set.

5. Line 24 mini (1¾-inch) muffin pan cups with foil baking cups. Spoon melted chocolate into prepared cups, filling evenly. Let stand until chocolate is very thick and partially set. Place trees upright in chocolate. Sprinkle tinted coconut over chocolate. Let stand until set.   *Makes 2 dozen place cards*

continued on page 208

Yule Tree Namesakes, continued

Butter Cookie Dough

¾ **cup (1½ sticks) butter, softened**
¼ **cup granulated sugar**
¼ **cup packed light brown sugar**
1 **egg yolk**
1¾ **cups all-purpose flour**
¾ **teaspoon baking powder**
⅛ **teaspoon salt**

1. Combine butter, granulated sugar, brown sugar and egg yolk in medium bowl. Beat at medium speed of electric mixer until well blended. Add flour, baking powder and salt; beat until well blended.

2. Wrap in plastic wrap; cover. Refrigerate until firm, about 4 hours or overnight.

Cookie Glaze

4 **cups powdered sugar**
4 **to 6 tablespoons milk**

Combine powdered sugar and enough milk, 1 tablespoon at a time, to make a medium-thick pourable glaze.

Icicle Ornaments

2½ cups all-purpose flour
¼ teaspoon salt
1 cup sugar
¾ cup (1½ sticks) unsalted butter, softened
2 squares (1 ounce each) white chocolate, melted
1 egg
1 teaspoon vanilla
Coarse white decorating sugar, colored sugars and decors
Ribbon

1. Combine flour and salt in medium bowl. Beat sugar and butter in large bowl at medium speed of electric mixer until fluffy. Beat in melted white chocolate, egg and vanilla. Gradually add flour mixture. Beat at low speed until well blended. Shape dough into disc. Wrap in plastic wrap; refrigerate 30 minutes or until firm.

2. Preheat oven to 350°F. Grease cookie sheets. Shape heaping tablespoonfuls of dough into 10-inch ropes. Fold each rope in half; twist to make icicle shape, leaving opening at fold and tapering ends. Roll in coarse sugar; sprinkle with colored sugars and decors as desired. Place 1 inch apart on prepared cookie sheets.

3. Bake 8 to 10 minutes or until firm but not browned. Cool on cookie sheets 1 minute. Remove to wire rack; cool completely. Pull ribbon through opening in top of each icicle; tie small knot in ribbon ends.   *Makes about 2½ dozen cookies*

Chocolate X and O Cookies

⅔ cup butter or margarine, softened
1 cup sugar
2 teaspoons vanilla extract
2 eggs
2 tablespoons light corn syrup
2½ cups all-purpose flour
½ cup HERSHEY®S Cocoa
½ teaspoon baking soda
¼ teaspoon salt
   Decorating icings

1. Beat butter, sugar and vanilla in large bowl on medium speed of mixer until fluffy. Add eggs; beat well. Beat in corn syrup.

2. Combine flour, cocoa, baking soda and salt; gradually add to butter mixture, beating until well blended. Cover; refrigerate until dough is firm enough to handle.

3. Heat oven to 350°F. Shape dough into X and O shapes.* Place on ungreased cookie sheet.

4. Bake 5 minutes or until set. Remove from cookie sheet to wire rack. Cool completely. Decorate as desired with icings.

Makes about 5 dozen cookies

*To shape X's: Shape rounded teaspoons of dough into 3-inch logs. Place 1 log on cookie sheet; press lightly in center. Place another 3-inch log on top of first one, forming X shape. To shape O's: Shape rounded teaspoons dough into 5-inch logs. Connect ends, pressing lightly, forming O shape.

Conversation Heart Cereal Treats

    2 tablespoons margarine or butter
   20 large marshmallows
    3 cups frosted oat cereal with marshmallow bits
   12 large conversation heart candies

1. Line 8- or 9-inch square pan with aluminum foil, leaving 2-inch overhangs on 2 sides. Generously grease or spray with nonstick cooking spray.

2. Melt margarine and marshmallows in medium saucepan over medium heat 3 minutes or until melted and smooth, stirring constantly. Remove from heat.

3. Add cereal; stir until completely coated. Spread in prepared pan; press evenly onto bottom using greased rubber spatula. Press heart candies into top of treats while still warm, evenly spacing to allow 1 heart per bar. Let cool 10 minutes. Using foil overhangs as handles, remove treats from pan. Cut into 12 bars. *Makes 1 dozen bars*

For a tasty Valentine's Day favor, wrap these bars individually in plastic wrap and tie them with pretty red and white curling ribbons. Write each recipient's name on a paper or lace heart and tie it to the package.

Shamrock Ice Cream Sandwiches

Butter Cookie Dough (page 208)
Green food coloring
1 pint ice cream or frozen yogurt, any flavor

1. Prepare cookie dough; tint desired shade of green with food coloring. Wrap in plastic wrap; refrigerate until firm, about 4 hours or overnight.

2. Preheat oven to 350°F.

3. Roll dough on lightly floured surface to ¼-inch thickness. Cut dough using 3½- to 5-inch shamrock-shaped cookie cutter. Place on ungreased cookie sheets.

4. Bake 8 to 10 minutes or until edges are lightly browned. Remove to wire rack; cool completely.

5. Remove ice cream from freezer; let stand at room temperature to soften slightly, about 10 minutes. Spread 4 to 5 tablespoons ice cream onto flat sides of half the cookies. Place remaining cookies, flat sides down, on ice cream; press cookies together lightly.

6. Wrap each sandwich in aluminum foil or plastic wrap; freeze until firm, about 2 hours or overnight.

Makes 6 to 8 ice cream sandwich cookies

Note: Filled cookies store well up to 1 week in the freezer.

Shamrock Ice Cream Sandwiches

Acknowledgments

The publisher would like to thank the companies and organizations listed below for the use of their recipes and photographs in this publication.

Duncan Hines® and Moist Deluxe® are registered trademarks of Aurora Foods Inc.

Eagle Brand®

Hershey Foods Corporation

© Mars, Incorporated 2004

National Honey Board

The J.M. Smucker Company

Texas Peanut Producers Board

Index

METRIC CONVERSION CHART

VOLUME MEASUREMENTS (dry)

1/8 teaspoon = 0.5 mL
1/4 teaspoon = 1 mL
1/2 teaspoon = 2 mL
3/4 teaspoon = 4 mL
1 teaspoon = 5 mL
1 tablespoon = 15 mL
2 tablespoons = 30 mL
1/4 cup = 60 mL
1/3 cup = 75 mL
1/2 cup = 125 mL
2/3 cup = 150 mL
3/4 cup = 175 mL
1 cup = 250 mL
2 cups = 1 pint = 500 mL
3 cups = 750 mL
4 cups = 1 quart = 1 L

VOLUME MEASUREMENTS (fluid)

1 fluid ounce (2 tablespoons) = 30 mL
4 fluid ounces (1/2 cup) = 125 mL
8 fluid ounces (1 cup) = 250 mL
12 fluid ounces (1 1/2 cups) = 375 mL
16 fluid ounces (2 cups) = 500 mL

WEIGHTS (mass)

1/2 ounce = 15 g
1 ounce = 30 g
3 ounces = 90 g
4 ounces = 120 g
8 ounces = 225 g
10 ounces = 285 g
12 ounces = 360 g
16 ounces = 1 pound = 450 g

DIMENSIONS

1/16 inch = 2 mm
1/8 inch = 3 mm
1/4 inch = 6 mm
1/2 inch = 1.5 cm
3/4 inch = 2 cm
1 inch = 2.5 cm

OVEN TEMPERATURES

250°F = 120°C
275°F = 140°C
300°F = 150°C
325°F = 160°C
350°F = 180°C
375°F = 190°C
400°F = 200°C
425°F = 220°C
450°F = 230°C

BAKING PAN SIZES

Utensil	Size in Inches/Quarts	Metric Volume	Size in Centimeters
Baking or Cake Pan (square or rectangular)	8×8×2	2 L	20×20×5
	9×9×2	2.5 L	23×23×5
	12×8×2	3 L	30×20×5
	13×9×2	3.5 L	33×23×5
Loaf Pan	8×4×3	1.5 L	20×10×7
	9×5×3	2 L	23×13×7
Round Layer Cake Pan	8×1½	1.2 L	20×4
	9×1½	1.5 L	23×4
Pie Plate	8×1¼	750 mL	20×3
	9×1¼	1 L	23×3
Baking Dish or Casserole	1 quart	1 L	—
	1½ quart	1.5 L	—
	2 quart	2 L	—